Wine Politics

Wine Politics

How Governments, Environmentalists,
Mobsters, and Critics Influence
the Wines We Drink

Tyler Colman

UNIVERSITY OF CALIFORNIA PRESS
Berkeley · Los Angeles · London

University of California Press, one of the most distinguished university presses in the United States, enriches
lives around the world by advancing scholarship in the
humanities, social sciences, and natural sciences. Its
activities are supported by the UC Press Foundation
and by philanthropic contributions from individuals
and institutions. For more information, visit
www.ucpress.edu.

University of California Press
Berkeley and Los Angeles, California

University of California Press, Ltd.
London, England

Library of Congress Cataloging-in-Publication Data
Colman, Tyler.
  Wine politics : how governments, environmentalists,
mobsters, and critics influence the wines we drink /
Tyler Colman.
    p.   cm.
  Includes bibliographical references and index.
  ISBN 978-0-520-25521-0 (cloth : alk. paper)
    1. Wine—Political aspects.   2. Wine industry.
I. Title.
HD9370.5.C65   2008
338.4'76632–dc22   2007032587

Manufactured in the United States of America

17   16   15   14   13   12   11   10
10   9   8   7   6   5   4   3

This book is printed on Natures Book, which contains
50% post-consumer waste and meets the minimum
requirements of ANSI/NISO Z39.48–1992 (R 1997)
(Permanence of Paper).

To Michelle and Zander, with love

Contents

Illustrations

Sidebars

Preface and Acknowledgments

When I recently told someone at a cocktail party about the subject of this book, he exclaimed, "Politics and wine! My wife and I debate that every night! I want red, and she wants white." This book is not likely to help resolve intrahousehold disputes over the evening's wine. Nor is it likely to satisfy those wondering about the wine preferences of presidents Nicolas Sarkozy (he says he's too busy to drink) or George Bush (a teetotaler since his fortieth birthday). Nor will it help those who seek hoary partisan orations from the well of the legislature disparaging other countries' wines (as members of the U.S. House of Representatives actually did in 2006). If you are looking for a drinker's guide to politics, this is not the book.

But if you are curious about the business and politics of just how that wine reached your table tonight, then this is the book for you. The politics of wine often operates out of the limelight. Celebrity winemakers may present themselves as all-powerful when it comes to making wine, but they too are subject to political forces. This book illuminates how distributors, mobsters, environmentalists, regulators, and critics all have a hand in producing, selling, and delivering the glass of wine we will drink tonight.

Previous books have told the story of wine in America. Others have examined wine in France. But no other book has ever looked at the two countries side by side, studying the different paths taken by winemakers in France and America to produce the quality wines we enjoy today. Battles with the soil and society have had different victors in each country, and these outcomes have influenced both the rise in quality and the broad social acceptance or rejection of drinking wine.

The term *politics* is often understood negatively, as an obstacle to a desirable result; that definition applies to the wine industry insofar as politics often reduces consumer choice in wine and raises prices. But in the United States, soon to become the world's largest consumer of wine, shifting fortunes and odd alliances have now led to groups aligning to produce some positive results for consumers. In France, the current story is less positive.

This book grew out of my PhD dissertation in the political science department of Northwestern University. I know it was the first—and perhaps it will be the last—dissertation on wine ever written in the department. But political economy frequently examines industrial sectors; and, fortunately for me, automobiles, machine tools, and semiconductors had already been thoroughly analyzed. The issue of quality was central to the project, as the market mechanism has difficulty in judging it.

Many people have helped me improve the book. The students in my wine classes in the food and wine program run jointly by New York University and the James Beard Foundation, as well as my loyal band of followers at the University of Chicago, have all helped make this a better book for a broad audience. They graciously read a few unadulterated dissertation chapters and then launched some hedonistic fruit bombs in my direction. My students have helped me translate the serious ideas from my academic research into prose and a tone that, I hope, goes down easily.

Many wine-industry participants from both sides of the Atlantic took time to talk with me about this book. I interviewed dozens of winemakers, civil servants, wine retailers, and environmental activists in France, the United States, and Brussels. I am grateful to them for enriching the book. I also consulted historical documents in archives in Paris and Bordeaux. The California Wine Oral History Series at the Bancroft Library, Berkeley, proved an excellent source for firsthand perspectives on wine production in California, particularly from the early participants.

Blake Edgar at the University of California Press and the two anonymous reviewers provided me valuable advice. Good wine drinkers Terry Halliday and Stephen Salerno both commented on chapters of their own free will. Patrick Comiskey provided useful and detailed comments on two chapters. And many other wine writers, particularly from the Wine Media Guild, gave me useful feedback along the way.

But I owe the greatest debt to my family. My wife, Michelle, undoubtedly knows far more about the politics of wine than she ever wanted to. And our son, Alexander, known early on as "bambino vino," makes me laugh every day. To them I raise my glass in a toast of gratitude, appreciation, and love.

CHAPTER 1

What Is Wine Politics?

The year 2005 was the best of times and the worst of times in Bordeaux. While some producers' wines fetched record prices, others went to the distillery to be turned into ethanol. The unusually dry summer gave way to sufficient rain to endow the vintage with a legendary quality. Château Haut-Brion, whose wines many critics called outstanding or perfect, priced its wine at $500 a bottle. Other châteaux doubled or tripled their prices from the previous year. Wine from Château Petrus, always among the costliest, sold for $2,000 a bottle—where it could be found. Retailers in London and Los Angeles could not get enough of it.

At the same time, however, many growers in the region were going out of business. In 2005, Bordeaux had about ten thousand wine-grape growers, roughly two and a half times the total in all of the United States. But that number was down from fifteen thousand a decade earlier. Producers of nondescript wine sold under the Bordeaux regional name could not sell their wine for consumption. Instead they sold 18 million liters of it to be distilled into ethanol for use as a fuel additive.

Granted, high oil prices have stimulated a search for alternative fuels. But wine? What had gone so terribly wrong that wine bearing the Bordeaux appellation—often viewed as synonymous with quality—was distilled so that cars could run on Cabernet? In a word, politics.

→>‹‹‹-

Jeff Lefevere, a wine consumer in Indianapolis, loves Sonoma Zinfandel. Whenever they are in the area, Lefevere and his wife visit A. Rafanelli, their favorite winery in the Dry Creek Valley. They would love to purchase the hard-to-find wines directly from the winery. But the winery won't send them wine. Are they debtors? Or under twenty-one? No, the reason for their blacklisting is simple: it is a felony to ship wine to residents of Indiana.

American consumers can buy computers and clothes directly from producers, cutting out the middleman. But many wine consumers must live with distributor monopolies that restrict the range of wines available. Lefevere describes the challenge in Indianapolis: because consumers "can't join wine clubs, can't ship back from wineries, can't buy off the Internet, you can't get on boutique winery mailing lists like Rafanelli—you just can't get access to a lot of the good stuff." Why is it often easier in America to buy guns, cigarettes, and pornography than it is to buy serious wine from California? In a word, politics.

–>–<–

In his home in Monkton, Maryland, Robert Parker swirls, spits, and scribbles. Although he grew up in dairy country in a household without wine, he is the world's most influential wine critic. His notes and scores can send the fortunes of wineries around the world soaring or plummeting. Parker has been called both the "emperor of wine" and the "dictator of taste."[1]

Parker's influence is so great that many wineries have styled their wines into what he calls "hedonistic fruit bombs" simply to please his palate. Why does one man's palate decide the winners and losers in the world of wine? Why are consumers at risk of confronting a sea of undifferentiated wine? In a word, politics.

–>–<–

Critics and commentators widely acknowledge the importance of the growing area and winemaking style in creating what ends up in the bottle. But, more than wine consumers realize, politics matters, too. Politics determines not only which grapes grow where, what can be written on the label, which wines are exported or imported, which wines are available in local stores, and how much a wine costs, but, perhaps most important, it also affects the quality of the wine in the bottle.

In this book I follow the travels that a bottle of wine takes from the vineyard to the dining-room table. Along the way it may encounter flying winemakers, humble *vignerons,* dull regulators, passionate activists, and powerful critics. I tell the neglected backstory of wine, which, as with Hollywood movies, can often be more interesting than the finished product.

While touching on issues as broad as dictatorship and democracy or international relations (the effects of showdowns in the United Nations, for example), battles over the politics of wine are more often fought on the ground—sometimes literally. Where are the lines of the best growing zones drawn? Will society stigmatize wine or praise it? How can consumers buy their favorite wines or discover new ones? Is a wine "made in the vineyard," as the industry likes to claim, or is it made in the lab and tested on focus groups for its consumer appeal? At stake in these battles are not only the livelihoods of those in the industry but also the prestige and the profits of an industry whose sales reach $25 billion in the United States alone.

Although the interplay between business and government affects winemaking and wine consuming everywhere, I focus on the two leading producer nations, France and the United States, and, within them, the prestigious regions of Bordeaux and Napa. As the leading producers of the Old World and the New World, respectively, these two countries and regions serve as models of their particular styles of wine production as well as of wine governance. The divergent paths they have taken hold lessons not only for each other but also for other countries and for consumers.

Both countries produce wines of outstanding quality. The notion that French wine is superior was effectively laid to rest thirty years ago, when American wines upstaged top French wines at a blind tasting in Paris. Since then, although their styles differ, both American wines and French wines have commanded stratospheric prices and received the highest scores from critics such as Robert Parker. But the trajectories of the two nations' wine industries have been dramatically different. In France, grapevines have occupied a natural place in the soil since before Roman times. Wine and France are symbolically intertwined, and that relationship transcends other social divisions. Wine was poured at Versailles as well as at peasants' tables. Americans, by contrast, have been trying to grow wine grapes for four hundred years and have only really succeeded in the past forty. And a widespread thirst for the fruits of the vine in the United States has developed only in the past fifteen years. American winemakers have had to overcome challenges from both soil and society. These legacies influence the wines we drink and will shape the future of the industry in both countries.

These separate paths are now converging. France, although still the world's most esteemed wine producer and its largest wine producer by value, has suffered setbacks. Exports have softened. Domestic sales have been crimped by the rise of antialcohol campaigns, which were a major obstacle to the development of quality wine in the United States in the early twentieth century. As a result, the French appellation system that governs the production of wine, including wines bound for the finest tables in the world as well as some of those now bound for the distillery, is being put under the microscope. At the same time America is on track to become the world's largest wine-consuming country in 2008, and wine is now being produced in all fifty states. And the notion of *terroir*, the French way of interpreting the characteristics of the growing area that lies at the very root of the appellation system, is being adopted and explored in the United States as well.

Looking at the two countries through the lens of the wine glass reveals paradoxes. We tend to think of France as a country whose economy is heavily regulated by the state, whereas the United States is the land of the free-market economy. Yet if that is the case, why does each of the fifty states have different rules for bringing in wine, as if each were a sovereign nation? The question is of particular importance for wine consumers outside California, where 90 percent of all American wine is made. It frustrates wine drinkers from Maryland to Montana who just want to be able to enjoy the wine of their choice. And why does France have strong and influential associations of wine producers, while in America they are weak? In his journey through mid-nineteenth-century America, Alexis de Tocqueville lavished praise on associational life in America while bemoaning the paucity of associations in his home country. Yet today, an abundance of French producers' associations may not be providing the vitality and social capital needed to improve quality sufficiently to enable their products to compete in a saturated global market for wine.

Will France be able to regain its lost luster? Are Americans doomed to drink standardized wine that is more expressive of the marketing department's recommendations than it is of the growing area? After reading this book, you may detect much more in a glass of wine than simply hints of blackberries, leather, or truffles on the palate; you will understand the convoluted path the wine took to reach you. This tale adds depth and complexity to every glass of wine by providing the story of who has tramped the grapes, both literally and metaphorically.

Chapter 2 traces the history of the wine industry in the United States and France, leading up to the crucial turning points in the 1930s that launched each country down its current path. Chapter 3 looks at the challenge of authenticating origins, the crisis facing the French wine industry, and the ways consumers may benefit from producers' pain. Chapter 4 examines the political foundation for the current laws on producing and selling alcohol in the United States as well as the changing pattern of alliances that sustains them, restricting the access of many American consumers to wines they want at prices they can afford. Chapter 5 considers questions of control: what are the effects of globally influential critics, flying winemakers, and new technologies? And what exerts the greatest influence in making the wine we find on retailers' shelves: the soil where it is grown, the winemaker, or a focus group? In a coda to the use of technology, chapter 6 looks at the increasing prevalence of "natural" winemaking, as many winemakers are turning over a new, greener leaf, prompted in part by environmental activists and in part by a blend of beliefs and marketing research. Understanding wine politics can bring the issues of yesterday and today into clearer focus and make for a more rewarding drink.

CHAPTER 2

Soil and Society

Wines in France and America before 1935

France had a reputation for producing fine wines well before the modern period. Ships laden with the wines of Bordeaux were traveling to Britain, Holland, and beyond centuries before the formal classification system for French wines was established in 1855. Their fame extended to the Americas: while serving as ambassador to France, Thomas Jefferson amassed a collection of French wines that he later shipped home. The challenge faced by French winemakers, then, was not how to make fine wines but rather how to maintain and protect their wines' reputation. The story of French wine from around 1850 to 1935 was one of boom and bust, brought on first by the development of the railroad and then by a phylloxera plague in the vineyards, fraud, and social upheaval. By the end of this period, the French wine market had split into two segments, a high end and a low end.

In America, by contrast, winemakers were struggling simply to produce acceptable wines. When Robert Mondavi opened his Napa Valley winery in 1966, he was in the vanguard of California winemakers seeking to produce world-class wines. American winemakers before them had battled with the natural environment, trying to coax suitable grapes to grow. When that battle was largely won, at least in California, they found themselves struggling against the powerful temperance movement over the place of alcohol in American popular culture. Without the advantages enjoyed by French producers—abundant wine-growing

areas and a thirsty population—winemakers in America had a rocky
start.

A CIVILIZATION OF WINEGROWERS

Wine has come to epitomize what is good and what is French. The tradition of growing and drinking wine has led to France's designation as
"the oldest daughter of Bacchus." One French writer has observed that
"Latin civilization is . . . a civilization of winegrowers"; another notes
that "the winegrowers are to French wine what the architects are to
our Cathedrals."[1] The French have almost always led the world in
their per capita consumption of wine, which peaked in 1900 at one
hundred liters per year.[2] So essential was wine to daily life that during
the First World War, French soldiers received a flagon of wine along
with food and weapons as standard battlefield issue.

"What does being French mean to you?" queried a survey for the
monthly *L'Histoire* in 1987. The reply "To like good wine" came in
fourth after "To be born in France," "To defend liberties," and "To
speak French." One commentator called wine "perhaps . . . a founda-
tional myth of the French nation. All in all, the map of wines of
France is nothing other than our national map. Wine, in short, is an
integral part of French civilization."[3] Some have further argued that
wine is a "civilizing" drink and that countries that make and enjoy
wine are "civilized."

Wine also has links to Christianity, particularly Catholicism.[4] Wine
and vineyards, often representing prosperity, figure more frequently in the
Bible than the milk and honey of the Promised Land.[5] In Genesis, Noah
plants vines after the flood. In the New Testament, Christ's first miracle is
to turn water into wine at the marriage in Cana. Wine is an essential ele-
ment of the Eucharist in the Catholic mass. In a more practical expression
of this link, during the Middle Ages Benedictine monks in the Loire, Burgundy, and Champagne regions maintained some of the finest vineyards
in Europe. Monks and missionaries setting out to evangelize the New
World brought wine as well as the word of God: the Jesuits brought vines
to Peru in the seventeenth century, and the Franciscans were instrumental
in the introduction of vines to California in the eighteenth century. The
connection with wine was not as strong in Protestantism, where wine and
alcohol have met with a more ambivalent reception.

In France, the strong association with national identity and the
church has given wine a cross-class appeal. Even so, different strata of

society have had different consumption patterns. Wine did not become a drink of the urban working class until the second half of the nineteenth century, when national rail networks made transportation easier. Before that, wine was a popular local drink in wine regions but a sign of wealth and status in Paris or Versailles, because only premium wines were worth the effort and cost of transporting them.[6] The symbolic importance of wine could be summed up, with apologies to Brillat-Savarin, in the expression "Tell me what you drink, and I will tell you who you are."[7] Indeed, the sociologist Pierre Bourdieu noted that knowing which wine to drink was a mark of distinction, showing whether the drinker had "luxury taste" or a "taste of necessity."[8]

Consumption patterns also vary considerably among different regions of the country. People in the north tend to drink more cider and distilled spirits, whereas those in the south drink more wine. Alcoholism in France is more common in the north, correlating with the higher consumption of spirits. Distinctive local and regional traditions of winemaking have been kept alive by wine tourism as well as by a practice of buying locally.

Wine, with a history perhaps longer than that of either spirits or beer, is traditionally not enjoyed on its own in France, but instead is mostly served with food. The classic French meal includes both wine and meat. As such, wine is considered a drink of moderation and has not (until recently) been associated with alcohol abuse, as beer and particularly spirits have been. Patterns of consumption vary by gender: men drink more than women, and men engage in more binge drinking.[9]

Despite high levels of consumption, the history of wine and distilled spirits in France has led to the view that "wine is not alcohol."[10] In the nineteenth century, the word *alcohol* referred only to beverages made by distillation. The French word *l'alcool* refers to the chemical substance that all fermented and distilled beverages contain, including wine. *Les alcools* refers only to distilled beverages, which are seen as manufactured rather than naturally produced. Thus wine, and particularly good wine, is distinguished from alcohol, although, like other spirits, it contains ethyl alcohol. Compounding this distinction is the belief that wine is good for health, whereas *les alcools* are widely considered harmful and the cause of debilitating dependency. Both the teetotaler *(le buveur d'eau,* or water drinker) and the drunkard *(le soûlard)* have traditionally been criticized for their extreme habits: the wine drinker, meanwhile, has been praised as a model of moderation.

Even into the twentieth century, doctors administered wine to their patients to fight alcoholism.

The Birth of the French Export Trade

Marriage and politics, rather than consumer demand, first brought the wines of Bordeaux to England. The marriage between Eleanor of Aquitaine and the soon-to-be king Henry II of England in 1152 started a trade relationship that has continued, with brief interruptions, to the present day.[11] The winegrowers of the region were given preferential tariffs, which greatly boosted their sales in England. The English trade also established Bordeaux as the center of wine exports, beating out La Rochelle, a coastal rival outside the English holdings. By the fourteenth century, Gascon wines, as they were known, were the most widely consumed in England, and fully a quarter of all wines from Bordeaux went in casks aboard ships to London. Quality was not particularly noteworthy under the three hundred years of English rule, as the wine barely lasted from one vintage to the next without spoiling. Not until the Dutch drained the swampy Médoc in the seventeenth century (thus creating better soil for the grapes), and keeping qualities were improved by the more widespread use of bottles and corks in the following century, did quality improve.[12]

Wine consumption was by no means universal in the patchwork of cultures that made up mid-nineteenth-century France.[13] A survey in 1850 found that three-fifths of the population did not drink much wine. Where wine was produced, it was abundant, but it was often so bad that peasants claimed it took three men to get it down: the one who drank, the one who held him, and the one who made him drink.[14] Although drunkenness was certainly not unknown, it was attributable more to brandy *(eau de vie)* than to wine. Because taxes on alcohol were high, the rural population drank mostly at holidays. The historian Eugen Weber suggests that the formation of a national army, particularly after the introduction of mandatory conscription in 1889, had much to do with the rise of drinking. Most drinking songs, for example, came from the army, not from a tradition of songsters in the local cafés.

The wines of Bordeaux differed from most other French wines. The region's strong tradition of exports to England and Holland was supported by the local merchants—the intermediaries between production and final sale known in French as *négociants*. Moreover, the easy access to the Bay of Biscay put the wines of Bordeaux at a significant advantage in the export markets compared to those from the Midi or the Rhône, which had to be shipped around the Iberian peninsula, or those from Burgundy, which had to make a long journey over land.[15] Coupled with political restrictions, such as prohibitions and taxes on the wines from up the Dordogne River, this geographic advantage put the Bordeaux wine producers in the unusual position of enjoying greater renown abroad than at home.[16] In turn, their expanded markets and their reputation for quality gave the Bordeaux producers access to more capital.

The *négociants* played a vital role in developing the wine exports of Bordeaux. In contrast to the owners of the vineyards, who were often aristocrats, these merchants in the city of Bordeaux were an emerging bourgeoisie and were often English or Dutch. Located along the banks of the Garonne River in the Chartrons district, they not only managed the trade between winegrowers and the foreign markets but also bought wine and provided blending and storage. Their market power derived primarily from the sheer volume of wines passing through their warehouses. They often used brokers, known as *courtiers*, to find wine for export and mediate the class divide between the nobility and the bourgeoisie. They sometimes even purchased properties, becoming *négociants-éléveurs*, or merchant-growers.

This market power was on full display when the *courtiers*, along with the local chamber of commerce, developed a classification scheme for Bordeaux wines in 1855, one that has firmly entrenched a hierarchy of producers in the region and still has inordinate influence. Napoleon III was an enthusiastic supporter of commerce and wanted to showcase the best French wines at the Exposition Universelle in Paris that year.[17] In response to his request, the brokers and the chamber of commerce of Bordeaux set up a hierarchy that classified sixty-one wines, all from the Médoc except for the wine of Château Haut-Brion in Graves.[18] Thus the five *crus* of Bordeaux were born. The four producers in the top tier were called first growths, or *premiers crus*, and their wines fetched the highest prices. Price was in fact the main factor in determining the producers' places in the hierarchy, although the brokers and chamber representatives also performed several tastings (and the categories were consistent with earlier attempts to classify the wines of the region). Another, two-tiered classification system emerged in the Sauternes for its sweet white wines, with Château d'Yquem taking the top honors in a category by itself *(grand cru supérieur)*.[19]

A crucial but often overlooked aspect of the 1855 classification is that it was the producers, also known as *châteaux* (see sidebar), that

ssified, not the actual vineyards. At first blush this approach
upport the notion of *terroir*, as it is based on the notion of a
..nd château surrounded by its vineyards. However, the classified
châteaux may have added or sold properties since 1855. Such changes
underscore that the ranking is attached to the château—a proto-
brand—and not necessarily to the growing area. Several classified
growths, particularly of the third, fourth, and fifth ranks, have either
gone out of business or been taken over by other producers. As one
author notes about Margaux: "The vineyards of Chateau Desmirail,
for example, have long been subsumed into Chateau Palmer, while
another Margaux Chateau, Ferrière, hardly exists as a third growth
wine (although the label is used by the owners of Chateau Lascombes),
and Chateau Dubignon-Talbot has not produced wine since the arrival
of phylloxera in the late nineteenth century."[20] Another author suggests that Château Palmer's low ranking may have been influenced by
the fact that it was in receivership in 1855.[21] Second-growth Rauzan-
Ségla was only revived in 1994, when the family that owned the
Chanel fashion house bought the property. And the grande dame of the
appellation, first-growth Château Margaux, made only middling wine
until the Mentzelo-Poulos family took over in 1978.

A significant problem with the ranking as it is applied today is that
it is based on a snapshot, and not a moving picture. Château Margaux,
for example, has purchased adjoining vineyards since 1855, thereby
presumably selling the lower-priced wines of a former competitor
under their own, more expensive label.[22]

Boom and Bust in the Nineteenth Century

Two changes led to the rapid expansion of wine production in France
in the mid-nineteenth century: the expansion of the railroad and
increasing demand from urban areas. Between 1857 and 1859 two key
rail lines opened, the Bordeaux-Sète in the Midi and the Paris-Lyon-
Marseille. Because Bordeaux already had access to the key export markets and the salons of Paris, these rail lines served to tap the enormous
productive potential of the Midi and bring it to the main urban areas,
creating a national market for wine. In 1862, the municipal council of
Narbonne in the heart of the Midi was delighted that "the wine that
passed through the coppers [stills for distillation into spirits] can now
be put on sale since the coming of the railway." In the Auvergne, the
persistent surplus of wine was even used to mix mortar.[23] The presence

WHY CALL IT A *CHÂTEAU*?

Although to most consumers the word *château* on French wine labels suggests centuries of elegance and viticultural tradition, it is mostly an early example of savvy marketing in the wine business. In the middle of the nineteenth century, *château* was an architectural rather than a viticultural term. The preferred term for a viticultural property of distinction was *cru*. An 1816 work by André Jullien, which devotes twenty-three pages to the vineyards of Bordeaux, uses the word *clos* for producer, never *château*. And, according to his 1822 classification, most of the top producers in the Médoc used *clos*: for example, Clos Lafitte, Clos Latour, and Clos Léoville.

In the celebrated 1855 classification of Bordeaux wine producers, the word *château* was used for only four wines out of the eighty *crus* from Médoc and Sauternes. Even Haut-Brion and Yquem did not use the word *château* (although both have magnificent buildings and long histories). Only four producers were then called *château*, although these included three of the four *premiers crus* (Lafite, Margaux, and Latour) from Médoc and one of the third (d'Issan). Thus, in a case of imitation being the sincerest form of flattery, almost all of the lesser wine producers traded up to usurp the term used by the first growths. From about 50 *châteaux* in 1850, the *Féret* (the essential and continuously updated French wine reference, first published in 1866) shows 318 in 1868, 800 in 1881, and 1,600 in 1908.

Finding a term that connoted the right blend of tradition, prestige, and quality was challenging. The French Revolution had demonstrated the dangers of using aristocratic titles, such as the old terms *terre noble* or *maison noble*. Moreover, *noble* did not fit, because some of the owners were *négociants* or bankers—members of the bourgeoisie, not the aristocracy. *Domaine* was initially considered too flat, and *clos*, as Philippe Roudie observes, was a term used mainly in Burgundy that lacked the suggestion of nobility and commercial appeal. The trick was to sound noble and traditional without using a blatantly false or potentially dangerous title. *Château* fit the bill perfectly.

For more on the history of *château*, see Philippe Roudie, *Vignobles et vignerons du Bordelais*, 1988, and Dewey Markham, *1855: A History of the Bordeaux Classification*, 1998, appendix 1.

---

of viable roads and rails radically changed the rural way of life through increased mobility and increased commerce.

If the railroad increased the national supply of wine, then the rise of cities increased demand. Living conditions in the middle of the nineteenth century were still poor, and wine represented a viable and sanitary alternative to contaminated drinking water.[24] Consumption rates climbed from 30 liters per capita in 1830 to 80 liters in 1875 and 100 liters in 1900. Quality mattered less than price. Wine was often sold at the urban markets out of large wooden barrels marked with the wine's alcoholic strength. A consumer who wanted to fill her jug with a liter of *onze*, or wine with an alcohol content of 11 percent, would pay less than someone who wanted a liter of *douze* (12 percent). After a crisis of powdery mildew that plagued the vines and decreased national production around 1850, the railroad pushed and the cities pulled wine from the Midi to slake the nation's newfound thirst.[25]

Between 1860 and 1875, French wine enjoyed a "golden age" of rising demand, favorable vintages, and increased access to new markets. National production in 1875 was 75 percent higher than in 1865. The area under grapevine cultivation expanded by 10 percent, and the average yield nearly doubled. Despite the vastly increased supply, wine prices and winegrower incomes held steady or increased across all regions during the period. Even in the Midi, the wealth of the winegrowers had become "legendary" as the latest fashions appeared on the streets of Narbonne and Béziers.[26] Thanks to a significant reduction in British wine tariffs in 1860, exports reached an all-time high in 1875, when they were France's second export earner, behind textiles. Further underscoring the importance of wine, the total tax on wine and on brandy distilled from it was the largest single contributor to the French annual budget, providing 15 percent of state revenue.[27] The national harvest of 1875 produced eighty-three million hectoliters (hL) of wine (equivalent to 1.3 billion 750 mL bottles), an amount not exceeded for one hundred years.

In 1875, however, the whole system collapsed under the shock of the phylloxera epidemic, which permanently altered the social structure of wine production. By the mid-1860s, some vineyard owners in the south noticed drying leaves on their vines, which subsequently died. They were surprised and frustrated when the chemical treatments for powdery mildew failed to stop the symptoms. Although it was immediately apparent that a serious new problem had taken hold, the cause and the cure took longer to discover.[28] In the meantime, the epidemic spread not only over most of France but also throughout Europe. Similar symptoms were found in Turkey, Austria-Hungary, Switzerland, Spain, and Italy between 1871 and 1879.[29]

By 1868 growers in Hérault, the Midi *département* at the epicenter of the crisis, had convinced public authorities of the need for further study. La Commission pour Combattre la Nouvelle Maladie de la Vigne identified the cause as a small, yellow louse that attacks the root of the vine. Because the obvious symptoms of phylloxera are rotting leaves and fruit rather than hard-to-see root damage, the findings of the departmental committee did not immediately carry the day. Several other theories were aired, including bad weather, overproduction, soil fatigue, and the wrath of God. But in 1869, a national commission quelled the speculation and declared phylloxera the cause. The preceding two decades had seen a dramatic increase in the number of plants and vines imported from America. Because the phylloxera louse had already been discovered in America, the panel concluded that it must have been inadvertently transmitted on vines imported from America.[30]

Despite this correct diagnosis and the importance of the issue (1.8 million citizens were engaged in growing wine grapes), an effective cure was slow to emerge. The Franco-Prussian War, subsequent reparations, and regime change no doubt preoccupied state officials. In 1870, the matter received national attention when the Chamber of Deputies in Paris announced the creation of a new high commission on phylloxera and a prize of twenty thousand gold francs for finding an efficacious method of fighting the disease. The commission received 696 proposals over four years, with some bordering on the absurd (burying a live toad at the root to attract the louse) and some mainly practical (digging cordons sanitaires to protect the unaffected areas). Most of the proposals came from chemists, and the solution taken most seriously was the application of sulfur to the vine. Flooding vineyards was commonly tried but impractical in many areas. Some growers, in desperation, even tried administering electric shocks. After four years, still no solution had emerged, and the prize money was raised to three hundred thousand francs. Phylloxera came to affect every winegrowing region, and was somewhat democratic in its impact insofar as it hit the fine vines as well as the inferior vines. The area worst hit was the relatively poor Midi. The effect was crippling in the *département* of the Gard, where the area under vine in 1875 declined by 57 percent from the previous year and by 83 percent over four years. Overall, the French area under vine declined by 17 percent from 1875 to 1885. This crisis cost the nation an amount comparable to the recently paid debt from the Franco-Prussian War.[31]

By the time of the International Phylloxera Congress in 1881, two groups, the "chemists" and the "Americanists," were proposing competing treatments. The chemists, who advocated sulfur treatments of the vines, had prevailed throughout much of the struggle but with mixed results. A growing group of scientists argued, counterintuitively, that because the phylloxera attacks the root of the vine, phylloxera-resistant American vines—probably the same species that had unwittingly brought the louse—should be imported and the French vines grafted onto them. Although the grafting treatment was showing some success, the practice was made illegal by a law in 1878 that forbade the importation of foreign plants, roots, and leaves out of a fear of exacerbating the problem. Ultimately, after trips to America by members of the French commissions and many debates with those advocating chemical solutions, grafting proved more successful. It was not a smooth nor speedy solution, as the American rootstock did not always take easily to the French soil. Almost a decade passed before advocates of grafting could achieve a total repeal of the ban on imported vines. During the time of the crisis and subsequent indecision, wine production fell 72 percent, to a nadir of 23 million hectoliters in 1889.

At the height of the phylloxera crisis, the growing demand for wine outstripped falling production, and prices rose. This shift gave producers a strong incentive to cut corners in production and led to a proliferation of "second wines," made by adding hot water and sugar to the fermenting residue in the casks used for the first wines. Some producers were even known to continue to a fourth or a fifth round of "stretching" the wine, yielding a product that did not resemble the first in any way besides simply containing alcohol.[32] In fact, because the only factor limiting the stretching of wine was the high price of sugar, the tax on sugar was reduced by 60 percent in 1885. In that year, the industry used 8 million kilograms of sugar; in 1886, the quantity rose to 26 million kilograms. The practice did not abate when the vineyards recovered. In 1899, when the harvest volumes had rebounded to almost twice the 1885 level, the industry used 39 million kilograms of sugar. The high levels of sugar in production later provoked a debate on the legal definition of wine.

After the grafting solution resolved the phylloxera crisis, replantings were eventually permitted in the afflicted areas, and planted land was given a special reprieve from taxes for four years, the time it takes for vines to mature and bear fruit. New plantings surged. The aftermath of phylloxera was perhaps as bad as the infestation: wages and prices fell, unemployment rose, and bankruptcies multiplied, leaving emigration as the only option for many. The *vignerons* were riding the boom-and-bust commodity cycle: the number of *vignerons* fell from 1.9 million at the height of pre-phylloxera demand to 1.5 million in 1892.

Although phylloxera reached Bordeaux and Burgundy, it affected winegrowing practices in the south most dramatically. Many of the hillside vineyards in the Midi were abandoned. The shift to the valley floors forced out other crops, established a monoculture of the vine, and boosted yields in the fertile soil. Large-scale holdings in the region came to control more production than small ones, making winemaking more capital-intensive while reducing unit costs, thereby forcing down the market price. Algerian production also increased significantly, flooding the mainland market with cheap wine. The severity of the crisis brought the concerns and troubles of growers to the ears of the government in Paris.

Fraud and Crisis: The Early Twentieth Century

As the French wine sector entered the twentieth century, not only were the winegrowers of the Midi facing plummeting prices and oversupply, but in Bordeaux and Champagne, producers attempting to protect their reputation for quality were confronting attempts at fraudulent use of place names. Different solutions, such as regulatory institutions and subsidies, were proposed for these differing problems. But these institutional approaches, whose foundations were built in legislation between 1905 and 1911 and fully established in 1931–35, successfully resolved the dilemmas of quality producers only while compounding the problems of the quantity producers, thus committing the two groups to seven long decades of antagonism and frustration.

In the Midi, declining prices and incomes caused desperation. As prices fall when production volumes rise, producers have a strong incentive to produce more to make up for the lost income. This response drives the price lower. The political responses to this commodity market cycle took two forms: grower organization and state policy. Growers in the Midi formed the first grower-owned cooperative in 1901. In 1905, this type of organization extended beyond local boundaries with the establishment of the Confédération Générale des Vignerons in 1905.[33] The CGV, whose membership grew rapidly, sought to root out problems of fraud—in this case, the addition of sugar to wine—and employed agents to investigate cases and bring them to trial, with surprising success.[34] This pattern of organization boosted the fortunes of the Socialist Party in the region, marking the beginning of century-long links between the viticulturalists of the Midi and the Socialist Party.

By 1907, growers in the Midi had sold their product below cost for five out of the previous seven years. The resulting economic hardship led to "the most violent peasant disorders that France had known since the Revolution," which compelled the state to take action.[35] In June 1907, agitated winegrowers staged a taxpayers' strike, demonstrators filled town squares, and several hundred mayors and town counselors sympathetic to the crowds resigned en masse. The demonstrations turned violent in a clash in Narbonne, a major town of the Languedoc. Troops fired into the crowd, and six people were killed. The French premier, Georges Clemenceau, then agreed to meet with the leaders of the movement.

The national government initiated several reforms in response to the structural crises of the wine industry and the pressure from its increasingly influential organizations. A 1905 law aimed to counter the fraudulent production of agricultural products and give consumers some legal redress. A branch of the finance ministry, best known by its short title, the Repression des Fraudes, was formed to enforce the new regulations. After the deadly clashes of 1907, the pace of reform accelerated: the national legislature passed laws that provided a legal definition of wine (it had to be fermented from fresh grapes), controlled the use of sugar, and established a policy requiring harvest declarations to provide information about the amount of wine produced and imposing controls on distribution *(circulation)*.[36] Although oversupply still threatened the stability of the market, the actions of the CGV, the legislative reforms, and good harvests after 1907 kept prices up until the onset of World War I. One scholar has suggested that the reforms of 1907 failed to sufficiently reduce the huge potential for grape production, for example by imposing yield controls or uprooting vines, because the winegrowers had a lingering hope that the region could experience another golden age.[37] As a result, the winegrowers did not demand and the state did not impose such measures. Nor did any group push to diversify the growing monoculture of grapevines, which increased the area's dependence on winegrowing.

If the main problem in the south was limiting supply, the main problem in the growing areas of Bordeaux and Champagne was limiting fraud, particularly the mixing of cheap, undifferentiated wines from Languedoc and Algeria into wines that were then sold as wines from Bordeaux or Champagne. Growers, producers, and *négociants* in these areas demanded a legal definition of origin. The first law governing

appellation d'origine was established in 1905, although it was a thin
and toothless law addressing only the issue of fake labeling, to be
enforced by the new fraud-control offices. After the riots of 1907 in the
Midi, quality growers in Champagne sought to further protect their
appellation by adding rules on local custom and a geographic delimitation of the grape-growing zone. In 1908, the Conseil d'État, a body of
the judiciary in Paris, handed down the boundaries for Champagne.[38]
Much to the surprise of the growers in the Aube *département,* their
vineyards were excluded, despite their claim that they had been the traditional capital of Champagne. Bad harvests in 1909 and 1910, and a
suspicion that imported wine from the Midi was being sold as Champagne, spurred a series of growers' protests in March and April
1911.[39] One of these involved a crowd of twenty thousand demonstrators; in another, the protesters turned their wrath on the *négociants*
suspected of importing and mislabeling wine and destroyed several cellars. After growers marched on Épernay, the traditional *négociant* center of Champagne, authorities in Paris dispatched fifteen thousand
troops to keep the peace, who remained there through the end of the
summer. The growers were not satisfied even after a decree mandated
another, less prestigious appellation, the Champagne Deuxième Zone.
Only a good harvest kept the fragile social peace in 1911. World War I
devastated the area and delayed a formal government response to the
disputes over demarcation.

In Bordeaux, both the producers and the *négociants* sought to protect the name of the region against any degradation through fraud. If
the experience of Champagne underscored the significance of geo-
graphical boundaries, then the experience of Bordeaux showed that
the process by which those boundaries were set was also important.
Whereas the Conseil d'État handed down the Champagne boundaries,
in Bordeaux the demarcations were proposed by local committees. A
first committee, dominated by elected officials, dithered and reached
an impasse. The minister of agriculture dismissed it and appointed
another, smaller committee composed of technicians, professors of
agriculture, and members of winegrowers' associations. This approach
seemed to bestow greater legitimacy on the boundaries, for the growers in excluded areas upriver did not protest in 1911 as they had in
Champagne. Nonetheless, fearful of violence, the new minister of
agriculture bounced the question of delimiting subregions in Bordeaux, a political hot potato, to the national Conseil d'État. But here,
too, government decisions on both boundaries and quality standards,

which arose briefly in parliamentary discussion, were delayed until after the war.[40]

-+->-<+-

By the 1930s, wine had reappeared on the policy agenda, and both the quantity and the quality issues were addressed in law. The abundant harvests of 1928 and 1929 in the Midi led the state to take the unprecedented action of purchasing F 250 million worth of alcohol distilled from wine. The severe market imbalance, combined with the onset of the depression, led the Chamber of Deputies to implement a serious reform. The *vignerons* of the Midi had their man in Paris: Édouard Barthe, the powerful deputy from Hérault in the Languedoc, who had led earlier efforts to classify wine as a permitted fuel additive. The Statut de la Viticulture of July 1931 introduced several market-stabilization measures to rescue quantity producers, particularly those in the Languedoc, from the commodity price cycles.[41] To reduce the quantity of wine on the domestic market, new labeling requirements and tariffs on wine from Spain were imposed in 1930. On the domestic side, unlike the reforms of 1907, the Statut sought to raise prices and limit overproduction. A portion of production in abundant years would be "blocked" or simply removed from the market. Even in normal years, wine was to have a staggered release onto the market. Furthermore, in a direct effort to reduce production, the law limited plantings, taxed extremely high yields, and, for larger producers (those generating more than four hundred hectoliters), introduced compulsory distillation of a portion of their annual production.

Conspicuously absent was any sort of a plan for promoting higher quality, an idea for which the Languedoc would have to wait another five decades. Under the Statut, small growers fared better than the large growers, as the legislation included several loopholes and exemptions from taxation. Growers in the Languedoc fared better than their counterparts in Algeria, the targets of particularly bitter parliamentary discussion and of publicity campaigns by the now-weakened CGV. This legislation was administered by a heavy state apparatus, including the interministerial committee on viticulture. The idea of a national office for wine was briefly floated. Clearly *dirigisme* (the tradition of economic management by the state) had become the mode of governance for bulk-wine production.

Although the Statut resolved the immediate market problems, the solutions bred further dependence on government intervention. Laurence McFalls colorfully summarizes the situation: "With the *statut,* the state took on the roles of both Savior and scapegoat. Thus, the history of the winegrowers' movement since 1935 has been one of a well-conditioned dog that bites the hand that feeds it."[42]

Concurrent with the wine statute, on a different legal and political track, came the formalization and strengthening of the appellations. On May 6, 1919, even before the signing of the Treaty of Versailles that formally ended World War I, the national legislature passed a law that made the judiciary again responsible for delimiting appellations. It also made the appellation a collective name not limited to one firm, and officially recognized local winegrowers' organizations, called *syndicats*. But it was efforts in the Rhône and Bordeaux that pushed quality onto the national political agenda. In the southern Rhône valley, several producers in the Châteauneuf-du-Pape area sought to improve quality after the war by replanting new vines of higher quality as well as by aging wines in barrels rather than large vats. Their efforts were systematically undermined by the local *négociants,* who would take a barrel of Châteauneuf, mix it with a barrel of cheap wine, and then sell both barrels as Châteauneuf. In response, the growers organized a local *syndicat*—a difficult task, as members not only had to pay dues to the organization but also sometimes had to modify their winemaking practices. They selected as their head the young, well-connected lawyer Baron Pierre Le Roy. Le Roy, who moved to Châteauneuf after marrying into a wine-owning family, had participated in the May 1907 demonstrations in the Languedoc. He had also won the Legion of Honor for his heroics in the war, shooting down twelve planes and being shot down twice. Le Roy's actions as head of the *syndicat* were controversial, and his own château suffered a boycott for the first four years after its creation.

After winning a regional court decision in favor of delimitation, the *syndicat* producers imposed more rules on themselves, with the goals of both protecting the collective name and increasing quality. The growers decided that Châteauneuf wines should have a minimum of 12.5 percent alcohol without allowing any *chaptalisation* (addition of sugar); growers had to reject 5 percent of the harvest through process as *triage* prior to fermentation; only approved grape varieties could be grown; and rosé wines were prohibited. Despite the local resistance, quality growers in other regions took a positive view of these standards, and some adopted similar controls for their *syndicats*.

Quality improvement in the Rhône coalesced with the Bordeaux approach, which sought further protection of place names in the law of 1935. As the growers of the Midi had their *député du vin*, Édouard

Barthe, the appellation producers had an ally in Joseph Capus. A former professor of agriculture, Capus represented Bordeaux in the Chamber of Deputies and served briefly as minister of agriculture in the 1920s. But it was as senator in the 1930s that Capus spearheaded the drive to regulate quality. The law of July 30, 1935, proposed a new, formalized appellation regime that became a model for the rest of Europe. The legislation gave wide-ranging powers to the producer *syndicats*. Producers, in association, could henceforth set their own rules on production, including limitations on grape varieties and yields, and a specification of minimum alcohol content. The legislation created a national committee of appellations, the Comité National des Appellations d'Origine (CNAO), which was made up of selected presidents of local *syndicats* as well as some representatives from the ministries of agriculture, finance, and justice. The CNAO, rather than the courts, would decide the boundaries of appellations. It was also charged with approving local appellation rules, providing technical assistance, and enforcing the rules. The budget came from a small levy (two francs per hectoliter) on the individual producers. Unlike the bulk winegrowers governed by the Statut, appellation producers set their own rules and policed themselves. As a result, many marginal producers were eager to join in order to escape the strict measures of the Statut. But the CNAO rebuffed attempts to dilute its authority, and appellation wine as a percentage of national production actually decreased in the years immediately following its formation.[43] The appellations were now legally known not simply as *appellations d'origine* but as *appellations d'origine contrôlées* (AOC), to emphasize not only the protection of the names against fraud but also the self-imposed measures to improve quality.

Between 1850 and 1935, the French wine producers split into two segments: bulk growers and quality growers. Each segment of the market had its own dynamics and forms of governance. Another split was regional: the south, with its ability to grow grapes abundantly, would wrestle with the curse of plenty for decades to come, whereas winemakers in Bordeaux, Burgundy, Champagne, and parts of the Rhône were able to build institutions to insulate themselves from the vicissitudes of the market.

ACROSS THE ATLANTIC: OVERCOMING ADVERSITY

In the United States, the story of wine had a different starting point, issues of struggle, and cast of characters. But it, too, reached a critical juncture in the 1930s. Wine's place in American policy and society has

been quite different from that in France. From its beginnings until Prohibition, the development of the U.S. wine industry took a circuitous
route, full of false starts, to end up arguably worse than it had been at
the outset.

Domestic wine production was slow to develop, despite some favorable public policies and friends in high places. As in France, United
States growers and producers did not control their own fates. In fact,
even early policies to encourage the growth of the wine industry failed
in the face of a harsh environment. Later, the industry suffered cyclical
fluctuations similar to those in France. The young United Sates had to
address a key question: should the production and consumption of
wine be supported by public policy?

Wine was not entrenched in U.S. national culture as it was in
France. The United States was founded by Protestants who did not
incorporate wine in their religious services as the Catholic Church did.
For a long time Americans, rich or poor, had no taste for wine at all.
Only in the second half of the nineteenth century, with the arrival of
European immigrants to the cities, did any sort of wine-drinking tradition develop. Nor did wine grapes hold the same significance in American agriculture as they did in France. At a dinner in San Francisco in
1891, President Benjamin Harrison served no California wines but
only French ones.[44] If any crops received "special" treatment in policy
and popular opinion, they were the feed and cash crops: wheat, corn,
tobacco, and peanuts.[45]

Wine was not, of course, completely unknown. While serving as
ambassador to France, Thomas Jefferson toured the wine regions of
France, as well as those of Germany and Italy, and had several cases of
wines shipped back with him to the United States. During his tenure as
president (1801–9), he served fine French wines at formal dinners. Jefferson sought to encourage domestic wine production, as tending vines
accorded with his view of the yeoman farmer in an agrarian republic,
as well as consumption; he kept wine taxes low. Although his own
efforts to grow vines at Monticello failed miserably (as did his campaign to make wine "the nation's drink"), his administration granted
land in Indiana for the construction of what became the first successful
commercial wine operation in the country (J. J. Dufour).[46]

Jefferson, like a few physicians and a handful of determined wine
growers, promoted wine as an alternative to the more plentiful and
harmful "ardent spirits."[47] In fact, for Jefferson, wine represented "the
only antidote" to the nation's "bane of whiskey"; he observed that "no

nation is drunken where wine is cheap."[48] He was not alone in this view. A Philadelphia physician authored a fiery pamphlet in 1784 denouncing the physiological effects of "grog" and spirits; he prescribed wine as a more temperate substitute. The grower Nicholas Longworth introduced viticulture and wine appreciation to the Ohio River valley in the 1840s with the aim of making it "America's Rhineland." Because he had already made his fortune (in real estate), Longworth did not seek to make a profit in wine but rather saw it as a way of introducing moderation to a nation that favored hard drinks, such as raw corn whiskey. However, like the original colonists in Jamestown, Virginia, long before him, he had difficulties in growing vines.

Whereas the French wine market was segmented by quality, in American wine production the key division was between producers and distributors. The extent and nature of government intervention was also markedly different in the United States: the state emerged as a powerful actor in the wine industry, passing legislation that variously prohibited, tarnished, and divided it.

Wine in the Colonies

Two hundred years before Jefferson, America had another head of state in favor of wine. James I, the English king at the time of the settlement of Jamestown in 1607, loved wine and abominated tobacco. In the years before Jamestown, the English had grown fond of foreign wine.[49] In his thorough history of wine in early America, Thomas Pinney demonstrates that those in London saw the American colonies as a way to expand not only the English holdings of gold but also the production of wine, silk, and olive oil. Colonial production of these commodities could reduce English dependence on imports from its traditional enemies, France and Spain.[50] After gold, wine and silk were seen as the most desirable products that the New World could offer.

King James, however, was disappointed with the goods coming back from Virginia. The colonists were struck by the abundance of native grapes. This profusion led to bold claims from promoters of the Virginia Company, one of whom wrote in 1609 that "we doubt not but to make there in few years store of good wines, as any from the Canaries."[51] The following year, the colonists made some wine from the local "hedge grapes" that was "strong and heady." The governor decided that, "sour as it is," they should send some back to England. At the same time, the tobacco that the king abhorred was starting to come back from America.

As tobacco rapidly proliferated in Virginia, a shocked King James dispatched eight Languedoc *vignerons* to the colonies in 1619. In 1621 there were ten thousand planted vines, with some *(Vitis vinifera)* having been brought over from Europe. In 1622, all the colonists received a manual on the production of wine and silk from the Master of the King's Silkworms. His instructions included crushing the grapes "with bare legs and feet" and adding water to native grapes, boiling the mixture, and letting it sit for several days in an effort to remove their distinctive flavor. One witness in that year reported that the colonists "laughed to scorn" at such instructions, for "tobacco was the only business."[52] Not only were the colonies failing to produce wine for export, but they could not even provide for their own consumption. The governor imposed price controls on imported wines, and the French winemakers were turned into scapegoats for the colonies' failure.

In France, the colonists' failure to make wine in America is often ascribed to a lack of tradition. Although it is true that the English lacked experience in viticulture, biology and entomology were probably more to blame. The imported grapes succumbed to local pests, and the abundant local grapes made undrinkable wine.

Vitis vinifera has been the vine for European wine grapes since before Roman times. This plant provided the leaves that Dionysus twined in his hair and the seeds that have been found in Egyptian tombs. The thin skin, sweet flavor, and high sugar content of the fruit make it well suited to wine production. A few particularly successful strains of the vinifera species have come to be known as the "noble" varieties, such as Cabernet Sauvignon, Pinot Noir, Chardonnay, and Riesling.

In North America, more than twenty native grape species existed at the time of the Jamestown colony.[53] The most common, *Vitis labrusca,* can survive cold winters and yields the hearty Northern Fox grape, which has a thick skin and a distinctive, sour flavor. The large, red Concord grape is the most common labrusca. Although it is widely used in jams and jellies to provide a "grapey" taste, the same flavor is undesirable in wine. Native vines are resistant to the voracious root-destroying aphid phylloxera, but vinifera vines are not. Bringing them to America was akin to a sacrificial offering to this minute louse. Americans would not fully understand the withering of their imported vines until the late nineteenth century, during the French struggle against phylloxera.

The Jamestown experience demonstrates a pattern that has repeated itself throughout the history of American winemaking, according to Pinney:

> First comes the observation that the country yields abundant wild grapes, followed by trials of the winemaking from them, with unsatisfactory results. Then the European grape is imported and tended according to the European experience; the early signs are hopeful, but the promise is unfulfilled: the vines languish, and no vintage is gathered. No amount of official encouragement, no government edict, can overcome the failure of the repeated trials, and after a time, men become resigned to the paradox of living in a great natural vineyard that yields no wine, though an enthusiast here and there in succeeding generations takes up the challenge again, and again fails.[54]

Early Signs of Success

At the end of the nineteenth century, after more than two and a half centuries of failures in American viticulture, growers in California succeeded within about fifty years of trying. California experienced many of the same problems as France, including a bout with phylloxera, a subsequent boom in plantings followed by a bust, and an effort to stabilize the market. Yet the dynamics, and particularly the public policy response, were quite different in California.

The rise of California as America's premier vineyard was swift. Although missionaries had brought a type of vinifera to the Spanish holding of California, plantings had been small. Even after California became part of the United States, the small local population limited the demand for wine. The discovery of gold in California radically changed the situation. In 1848 the state had 4,000 inhabitants; four years later it had 250,000. Many of these immigrants came from southern Europe and brought with them an appreciation of wine.

The dominant vine was the Mission vine, which grew well in California's Mediterranean-type climate but produced an indelicate wine. The phylloxera louse that had tormented the early colonists had not crossed the Rocky Mountains, so the vinifera vines grew well. In 1869 the transcontinental railroad was completed, linking California to the East and opening new markets for California wine.[55] New plantings and vine imports rose sharply to keep pace with demand.

In 1873, phylloxera struck the California vineyards. It was not as devastating as the outbreak in France because different soil and lower humidity slowed its spread. Nonetheless, the onset of phylloxera, coupled with a recession in 1873, severely shook the industry. Forced to sell their wines below cost, producers were driven out of business. Only 45 producers remained in 1880, compared with 139 in 1870. Unlike the government of France, the state government did not attempt to intervene or investigate: growers had to use trial and error to combat the pest. Grafting onto phylloxera-resistant root stock quickly proved successful in California.

During the resulting wine shortages, both producers and the merchants engaged in corner cutting and fraud. Because there were few recognized growing regions or restrictions on the use of their names, the main types of fraud were the labeling and sale of good American wines as French wines and the sale of cider, colored and flavored with chemicals, as California white wine. Only a few county-level wine-growers' associations emerged in resistance to this fraud. A proposal for a national pure-wine law dissolved in conflict between Eastern growers and Californians over the addition of sugar. In California, the long, hot summers produced high levels of natural sugars in the grapes, and growers did not need to add sugar as they did in the East.[56] In 1887 the California legislature passed a state law declaring that wine must be made from grape juice without added sugar.

The 1880s brought bountiful harvests. As more acres came under vine and production volumes increased, prices dropped. As in France, three main strategies for resolving the commodity-pricing crisis emerged: increasing national consumption, increasing quality, and controlling supply.[57] Although the proponents of increased consumption saw in wine the Jeffersonian ideal of moderation and yeoman democracy, their position did not prevail. Despite the promise of new urban markets offered by the coming of the railroad, per capita consumption remained low. Large swaths of the population drank no alcohol at all.

A few producers focused on improving quality by making wines in the Bordeaux style with Bordeaux varieties, a move that prompted a massive uprooting of the inferior Mission grapes. In the 1880s and 1890s, Napa Valley wines collected prizes at several international exhibitions.[58] Capital poured in, and some of it was aimed at quality wines. George Hearst, a U.S. senator and the father of William Randolph Hearst, used his mining fortune to buy a large vineyard in Sonoma County. Leland Stanford, a former governor of California who had made a fortune in the railroads, sought to make quality wines in the name of moderation.[59] In arid Tehama County, north of Sacramento, Stanford purchased a massive amount of land. In 1881 he planted what was described as the "largest vineyard in the world," with 2.6 million vines on 3,500 acres, and built an enormous winery with two acres of cellars.[60] Poor site selection, however, doomed the venture, as the grapes did not yield a quality wine. Stanford shut the winery down. Running counter to his original intention, the entire production was distilled into brandy.

While private efforts to improve quality were moving haltingly forward, the dearth of industry associations was striking. One organization of producers that did emerge, albeit under state auspices, was the Board of State Viticultural Commissioners. Originally established in 1880 to address the phylloxera crisis, the board favored business interests, as all nine members were producers. The board advocated promoting quantity over quality, arguing that higher yields would produce better returns. In opposition to this view stood the viticulture department at the University of California at Berkeley, also founded in 1880, dedicated to the improvement of the state's wine. Professor Eugene Hilgard planted an experimental vineyard in Berkeley and pushed California winemakers toward improving hygiene and quality. Hilgard was often in conflict with the commercially oriented board until it was abolished in 1895.[61]

When boosting demand and quality failed to resolve the crisis, what succeeded was controlling supply: not with state action, as with the French Statut de la Viticulture, but through a private-sector monopoly. By 1894, the California industry was in desperate shape because of overproduction, falling prices, and a national recession. In 1894 several San Francisco merchants formed the California Wine Association (CWA), a corporation that sought to regulate the market through vertical integration of private companies, as was the trend in other industries, such as oil and steel. A rival group formed an alternative corporation, but after only two years of conflict, which the newspapers dubbed a "wine war" (though there were neither deaths nor clashes), the rival group went out of business and sold its assets to the CWA.

It was clear from the action of the "wine trust," as critics called the CWA, that the CWA stranglehold on the industry was not compatible with improving quality.[62] As the CWA controlled the dominant share of production, it effectively set the price for the state. The corporation brought grapes into a central winemaking and bottling facility in San Francisco and then sent the wine all over the country, particularly to cities in the Midwest and East where wine was popular with European immigrants. Although the CWA acquired some of the premier wineries in Napa Valley, it did not label the wines separately. It offered mostly red or white wine, but it also produced an increasing quantity of fortified wines that seemed less like table wines and more like distilled spirits, the bane of the temperance movement. By 1900, the volume of California wine production reached had 20 million gallons (about 1 percent of the French national production that year), up from 4 million in the 1870s. By 1910, a CWA pamphlet boasted that it had the largest vineyard acreage, crushed more grapes annually, and operated more wineries than any other wine concern in the world.[63]

The boom-bust cycle in California was thus broken through the creation of a private monopoly. Wine was not linked to the national identity, as in France; it was not as large a contributor to the national economy; and the phylloxera scourge was not as devastating. As a result, there was little pressure for the state to intervene. Instead, the prevailing support of trusts let authorities tolerate the monopolists, at least until the arrival of Prohibition. Because the CWA was a volume producer not particularly interested in quality, the wine market did not split along quality lines as it had in France.

The Temperance Movement

The temperance movement that emerged in the mid-nineteenth century had an enduring effect on the industry's governance and quality. "Abstinence movement" might have been a more appropriate name, as that was the organization's ultimate goal. Its adherents' view that alcohol consumption should be banned was based on a combination of religious doctrine and rampant evidence of the hardships that liquor could cause. The influence of the temperance movement fanned across America as the phylloxera scourge had spread across France. Portland, Maine, was the first city to vote itself "dry" in 1843; in 1844 the Oregon Territory passed a law forbidding the sale of spirits. In 1851, Maine passed a law prohibiting all intoxicating liquors. The "Maine Law" became a model for convinced prohibitionists throughout the country (and the leading example of American intolerance to liberals throughout the world—John Stuart Mill, for example, gravely condemned it in *On Liberty*).[64] Evanston, Illinois, declared itself dry from the time of its founding by Methodists in 1855.

The Civil War was a setback for the temperance cause, but it was also the foundation of a set of bizarre relationships between alcohol producers and the state. To raise money for the war effort, Congress imposed a licensing fee on liquor retailers and a tax on the production of beer, spirits, and wine (the fee on wine was five cents per gallon). Although the measure succeeded in boosting the Union's treasury, it had two unintended consequences.[65] First, it legitimated the alcohol industry's existence and brought many of its activities above board through more accurate tracking. Second, it established a precedent for viewing the alcohol industry as a source of state revenue. After the war was over, the alcohol taxes remained in place, although at lower rates.

After the Civil War, the temperance movement gained strength and ambition. The idea of amending the Constitution to achieve a national prohibition was first considered in 1876. But the idea foundered until it had more organizational and political muscle. That was provided by the Women's Christian Temperance Union, founded in 1874 in Evanston, Illinois, and directed by Frances Willard, and the Anti-Saloon League, founded in 1895, which became the major force in pushing the Dry cause. The Drys (as temperance advocates were dubbed), along with women's suffrage groups, were the most important social movement of early twentieth-century America.

A campaign for a national prohibition was preceded by state-level action. By 1919, thirty-three of the forty-eight states had passed their own prohibition measures. These decisions were made possible by a 1913 act of Congress that permitted states to enforce their own laws on interstate commerce in alcohol, a position that appeared to conflict with the interstate commerce clause of the Constitution. In the succeeding Congress, a motion for a prohibition amendment failed to achieve the required two-thirds majority. But on a second try, in August 1917, the Senate passed a prohibition amendment. In December the House passed the amendment by a sufficient margin. The rhetoric was highly charged, as the United States was by then at war. A federal food-preservation act gave "men the opportunity to identify temperance with Americanism and to identify the liquor interests with treason."[66] Within just over a year, the required two-thirds of the states had ratified the amendment: constitutional prohibition had been achieved. The country embarked on what President Hoover called the "noble experiment."

The next task for the legislature was to turn the vague language of the Eighteenth Amendment into a specific framework for enforcement. At particular issue for the wine industry was the official interpretation of the phrase "intoxicating liquors." Would the Jeffersonian (and French) position that wine was a drink of moderation, and its different methods of production and consumption, exempt it from complete prohibition? Or would the presence of ethyl alcohol consign it to the same category as the "Demon Rum" that the Drys so fervently opposed? In the end, in formulating the National Prohibition Act (better known as the Volstead Act after its sponsor, Representative Andrew Volstead), Congress left a loophole for wine.

The Volstead Act permitted the manufacture of "non-intoxicating" cider and fruit juice for home consumption. But this was not a concession to the wine sector. American farmers in the East had long made hard cider and had even won opt-out clauses under some of the state prohibitions, such as Virginia's. While "non-intoxicating" was not clearly defined, intoxicating levels of alcohol were defined as greater than 0.5 percent. This loophole was to have significant consequences, some intended and some unintended, for the regulation and production of quality wines in the United States for decades to come.

Prohibition's Paradox

The arrival of Prohibition in 1920 was a severe blow for the wine industry, but the "non-intoxicating" loophole tempered the shock. Although the number of wineries in California fell from more than 1,000 to about 150, three legal loopholes enabled wine production to continue. First, wineries were allowed to produce wine for sacramental use in churches. Second, wine was allowed for medicinal purposes. The limited number of wineries that did produce continuously under Prohibition owed their survival to these two exemptions. The third and most important loophole concerned home production. According to Section 29 of the Volstead Act, each household was permitted to produce up to two hundred gallons of "non-intoxicating" fruit juice for consumption by members of the family over eighteen. This production could not be sold or bartered and was strictly for home use. The legal production of homemade wine was a boon for the grape growers. Although the number of wineries declined dramatically, the acres under vine doubled between 1919 and 1927 as grapes were transported across the country for home vintners. In fact, wine consumption actually increased under Prohibition.[67]

The enforcement provisions of the Volstead Act were very weak. Enforcement officers were from the Treasury Department, not the Justice Department. Having Treasury officers enforce the law made sense when there was an excise tax to collect, but as the entire trade, or "traffic" (as the Drys called it), was eliminated, it generated no revenue. Thus enforcement was a continuing problem in state and local prohibitions. As Pinney observes of the state laws preceding national Prohibition, "There were few means for enforcing [them] and even less will to do so."[68] The systematic disregard for the laws and their slack enforcement led to a sharp divergence between the law on the books and the law in action. Indeed, at the beginning of national Prohibition in 1919, there were only 1,512 officers to enforce the laws across the country, and their number never exceeded 3,000 during all of Prohibition.[69] As a result, the overstretched enforcement officers focused on the most flagrant violators, the "rum runners" of organized crime, and not the home producers.

As enforcement officers turned a blind eye to home production, the wine-grape industry flourished. Boxcars of grapes traveled east from California. A small industry sprang up providing products such as bottles, corks, labels, presses and crushers to home producers. Bob Trinchero, who later became one of California's most successful wine producers, recalled that his family set up a speakeasy in Lake George, New York, in 1919 that sustained the family until Repeal. They imported boxes of grapes by rail to the region, which had no local grapes, and made them into wine in the basement of their hotel, the Paradise Inn. They found winemaking to be a "very lucrative" niche, as well as a safe one, because the gangsters were more interested in beer and spirits. Avoiding the wrath of the gangsters was more important than escaping the law-enforcement officers because "the law was nothing. . . . It was the gangsters who would fill your house with bullets."[70]

By the late 1920s, firms sprang up seeking to capitalize on the "fruit juice" loophole not only through selling products, but also by providing services. The most audacious of these was Fruit Industries, Inc., which aggressively marketed its product, Vine-Glo. Fruit Industries was in fact the California Wine Association, or "wine trust," under a new corporate organization. Fruit Industries would deliver grape concentrate to the home and subsequently supervise its fermentation into wine and then bottle it. It advertised, "You take absolutely no chance when you order your home supply of Vine-Glo which Section 29 of the National Prohibition Act permits you."[71] As this was stretching the letter of the law, the company hired none other than Mabel Walker Wildebrandt, known as the "Prohibition Portia," away from the Justice Department, where she had prosecuted violations of the Volstead Act for eight years. Even though Fruit Industries really only got under way in the twilight of Prohibition, it was still too much of a stretch for the Justice Department, which threatened suit, and Vine-Glo was removed from the market in 1931.

While enforcement issues chipped away at the popular support for Prohibition, the onset of the Great Depression provided a strong economic argument for a national repeal. Repeal, it was argued, would create both more jobs and higher tax revenues.[72] In 1928, an election year, Prohibition survived an attack in part because the economy was still strong. But by 1932 neither major party made support of Prohibition a part of its platform. The same switch was also apparent in congressional hearings. In 1926, witnesses against Prohibition were hard to find, and those who did testify couched their opposition in the logic of personal liberty. By the 1930 hearings on the subject, unions took a strong stand against the amendment on the grounds that its repeal would put men back to work. The same was true in the 1932 hearings, when the Glass Blowers Union, the Lithographers Union (which made bottle labels), the Allied Association of Hotel and Stewards' Associations, and other groups made direct appeals for Repeal. Popular support and elite support began to erode for the Dry movement. In 1926 the prominent DuPont family swung to oppose the Drys. By 1932, stalwarts of moral reform such as J. D. Rockefeller and S. S. Kresge left the movement. Shrinking federal revenues and a lack of jobs combined with poor enforcement to fatally doom Prohibition.

Passage of Repeal was swift after Franklin D. Roosevelt won the 1932 election in a landslide. On December 6, 1932, John J. Blaine of Wisconsin drafted a joint resolution calling for the submission to the states of the Twenty-first Amendment, which would void the Eighteenth. Both houses had adopted it by February 21, 1933, and it was forwarded to the states. One of the new president's first acts after inauguration was to ask Congress to modify the Volstead Act to legalize 3.2 percent beer. Within nine days, "3.2 beer" became legal. Some pundits said it would take years for the necessary two-thirds of the states to act on Repeal, but on December 5, 1933, Utah became the thirty-sixth state to ratify the Twenty-first Amendment (it actually delayed the vote for a month so that it would be the thirty-sixth and deciding state). When President Roosevelt signed the bill, he ended thirteen years, ten months, and eighteen days of the "noble experiment."[73]

The Politics of Repeal

The provisions of Repeal led to wide variations in state laws governing the production and consumption of alcoholic drinks. The loophole that

Congress left the wine industry arguably did it more harm than an outright prohibition would have done. With a complete ban, wine could
have gained status as a drink of moderation after Repeal. As it was, the
quality of wine had been so degraded (by the dismal efforts of home
winemakers and the loss of professional skills and winemaking infra-
structure) that it took the industry almost fifty years to recover.

Even though the swift passage of the Twenty-first Amendment was a
crushing political failure for the Drys, they influenced legislation governing Repeal. And, having lost the national prohibition, they pushed
for continued state-level prohibitions. Section 2 of the Twenty-first
Amendment stipulated the authority of individual states: "The transportation or importation into any State, Territory, or possession of the
United States for delivery or use therein of intoxicating liquors, in violation of the laws thereof, is hereby prohibited." Thus, even though
Prohibition at the federal level lasted for only about fourteen years,
prohibitions existed at the state level for more than a century, from
Maine to Oklahoma, and even in some states whose representatives
had voted for the federal repeal.

Although several large states, such as New York, California, and
Illinois, repealed their prohibition laws immediately after the federal
repeal, many did not. Oklahoma did not repeal its prohibition until
1959. At the municipal and county levels, prohibitions lasted even
longer (and many still remain in place). In a series of opinions written
by Justice Louis Brandeis, the Supreme Court maintained that all
states, not just dry ones, had the power to regulate alcohol trade within
their borders.[74] State taxes on wine therefore varied widely, ranging
from one cent per gallon in California to $1.75 in Florida. Some states,
such as Pennsylvania and Utah, retained a monopoly on the retail sale
of alcohol; others regulated the opening hours of shops, often prohibiting the sale of alcohol on Sundays, and imposed rules about where different types of alcohol could be purchased. The legacy of Prohibition
was a chaotic patchwork of state regulations for producers and consumers to navigate. (Chapter 4 examines more closely the forces that
keep these laws alive today.)

At the federal level, the Drys continued to exert some power over
wine policy. The Roosevelt administration sought to help revive the
domestic wine industry. It established an experimental winery at the
Department of Agriculture facility in Beltsville, Maryland, and another
in Mississippi.[75] However, an influential Dry congressman on the
House Appropriations Committee threatened to block the entire

budget for the Department of Agriculture unless the wicked "fermentation" projects were terminated. Rather than jeopardize the whole budget, the Department of Agriculture conceded, closing the unused experimental station, selling off the machinery, and scrapping the plans for the second station. The department completely withdrew from any initiative having to do with winemaking for the next several decades.

This confrontation in the House early in Repeal had lasting effect on the governance of the wine sector. Wine came to be seen not as an agricultural product, but rather as alcohol. The lingering anxieties among policy makers were so great that the federal government scaled back its role in the wine industry and largely limited its involvement to tax collection. With the exception of California, the states did little to encourage production and strongly controlled distribution. Most states rigorously separated the production, distribution, and final sale (in stores or restaurants) of alcoholic beverages. In the name of moderation, producers were not allowed to own retail outlets (as they had done with saloons in the American West, and as brewing companies still own some English pubs today): firms in the post-Repeal period were allowed to operate in only one of the three spheres. Such regulation was meant to prevent producers from exerting excessive market power but instead had significant unintended consequences for consumers and members of the wine trade.

Home winemaking dealt a severe blow to the quality of American wines. Inexperienced home winemakers were more likely to choose grapes because they looked good (even after making the transcontinental journey in a boxcar) than for their winemaking potential. As a result, buyers often opted for the native varieties. After Repeal, the vineyards had to be replanted with quality grapes. A further obstacle to quality production was the lack of trained winemakers. Home winemaking, especially in the later stages of Prohibition, became a large-scale, unregulated, and unskilled affair. Practices such as the excessive use of sugar (for raising the alcohol level) and water (for stretching the final product) abounded. Wine had lost much of its claim to distinctiveness.

➝➤⫷⫸

In France, winemaking came easily. Vines grew abundantly, and French consumption expanded from the grape-growing regions to become a national tradition. Wine became central to the image of being French. In America, by contrast, vines found a hostile natural environment that took centuries to overcome. Just as the sparks of quality winemaking started to glow brightly at the end of the nineteenth century, temperance snuffed them out, degrading not only the vineyards but also, and more important, consumers' perception of wine.

The next chapter picks up the story of the French appellations today. After operating smoothly for a few decades, the appellation system became suddenly overburdened in the 1980s. Calls for reform rang out for the appellation wines; and, sadly, shots rang out from the Languedoc as violence again seemed for some the only way out of the crisis.

Chapter 4 resumes the story of wine in the United States. Prohibition and its aftermath gave the industry a hangover that took decades to recover from; in fact, its effects are still being felt. In spite of that legacy, quality also improved (thankfully), as American wines climbed onto the world stage.

CHAPTER 3

Authenticating Origins

Appellations and Quality

"We don't make wine to please consumers," a senior wine-industry official told me in his Paris office in 2000. "We make wines that are typical of their *terroirs*. Fortunately for us, consumers like them."[1]

This is one way to make wine—add a dash of arrogance. However, within a few years of his remark, this strategy was showing distinct limitations. Exports had dropped sharply, and the domestic market had also shrunk. The wines might still have expressed the qualities of the *terroir*, or growing area, but consumers no longer seemed to like them as much. A closer look at the recent downturn reveals a segmented market. The high-end producers have been able to navigate the choppy seas of the past few years successfully, producers in the middle tier less so; and for the low-end producers, the situation has been dire.

Bordeaux is known mostly for trophy wines that can fetch several hundred dollars a bottle on release. The critic Robert Parker refers to Bordeaux as a touchstone for quality. But Bordeaux is actually a vast region that produces everything from the high-end *grands crus* to bulk wine, sold in huge containers. With about 10,000 growers tending 300,000 acres of vines that made enough wine to fill 1.6 billion bottles in 2005, there is clearly more wine than can be sold at exalted prices. In fact, in 2005 growers in the region accepted funds to uproot some vineyards and, even worse, sent the equivalent of two million cases of wine to the distillery, where it was turned into a fuel additive. Recently, several hundred wine growers have been abandoning winemaking in the region every year.

Clearly the appellation system is not operating as intended. But even though it is sputtering, the system remains important for a number of reasons. The first is that it does produce exceptional wines: some of the finest wines in the world bear an appellation name. What sort of controls are applied to the production of France's best wines? And who makes and enforces the rules?

Second, the system is expanding despite its shortcomings. Even in the face of the national decline in wine consumption, appellation wines have grown to account for 55 percent of all wines produced in France by volume and an astonishing 81 percent by value. Third, even though the appellation system appears broken today, it has been the prevailing mode of managing quality wine production in France for the last seventy years; and, in the absence of any consensus on an alternative system, it remains the status quo. Fourth, the French appellation system has served as a model for other countries, notably the *denominazione di origine controllata* and *denominación de origen controlada* systems of Italy and Spain, which govern most of their quality wines. And it has extended to gourmet foodstuffs, with the producers of some distinctive French cheeses, olive oils, nuts, and chicken adopting the structure as well.

Many commentators, particularly in America and Britain, have an imperfect understanding of the system and perpetuate misconceptions about it that should be corrected. British wine writers often refer to the system as simply *appellation contrôlée*, thereby subtly reinforcing the "control" aspect and omitting the essential concept of "origin." The author of a recent book on Bordeaux mistakenly referred to INAO (Institut National des Appellations d'Origine), the national appellation organization, as "a division of the Ministry of Agriculture," and a leading British wine magazine called it "government run."[2] These observers confuse the appellation rules with the state structuring of the French economy.

In fact, the governance of quality winemaking defies conventional interpretations of French law and culture. Since the time of Jean-Baptiste Colbert, the controller general of finances of Louis XIV, the state has played a decisive role in economic governance. Indeed, some commentators suggest the French economy is still statist, although most political economists concede that since the Socialist U-turn in 1983, privatization and flexibility have shaken that image. For an example of a more liberal—that is to say, less state-controlled—economy, the French have historically looked to America, as did Alexis de

Tocqueville in his homage to the vibrant associational life that he found in mid-nineteenth-century America.

However, examining France through the lens of the wine glass would have made de Tocqueville proud—at least until the latest crisis. Surprisingly, voluntary associations have taken the lead in governing the production of quality wine. The fact that more Americans are "bowling alone," in the words of the social critic Robert Putnam, makes this finding doubly surprising. Admittedly, quality winemaking is more tightly regulated in France than in America (or Australia or Argentina, for that matter). But what escapes many English-speaking observers is that those regulations are imposed by the producers themselves, not by "heavy-handed regulators."[3]

In light of the current crisis (and a lot of grumbling), why are producers still signing up for the appellation system? Why is it so rare for a producer to quit the system, unlike, say, those in Italy, where producers essentially quit the *denominazione* system en masse to create the category of Super Tuscans?

-+->-<-+-

André Lurton, born in 1924, has worn a lot of hats. The Bordeaux winemaker holds the highest civilian honor in France, the Legion of Honor, and is a member of the Knights of the Agricultural Order of Merit. He owns almost a dozen châteaux in Bordeaux, including La Louvière and Bonnet. His grandfather owned a distillery, and his father came to own several wineries, including the second-growth Brane-Cantenac in Margaux. André's two younger brothers and their numerous children own various other châteaux. André has seven children, but only his sons Jacques and François have become château owners, with their JFL Wines. André claims that, unlike the wealth of many château owners who made fortunes in construction, banking, or insurance, "all the money that I have made comes from the wines I have produced and sold."[4] He became active in the politics of the region in the mid-1940s, when he founded the local farmers' union. And he was the mayor of Grézillac, his hometown in Bordeaux, for forty years.

Lurton knows the rules and procedures for the appellations well, as he has not only helped to found but also been the president of two of them. In the 1950s, he helped revive the growers' syndicate that had been dormant since the 1920s in the Entre-Deux-Mers, a forgotten swathe of rolling farmland situated on the broad plains between the region's two rivers, the Garonne to the south and the Dordogne to the north. But his more recent and more quality-oriented campaign was to create the appellation Pessac-Léognan, established in 1987 after twenty-three years' effort. That's a long time even by appellation standards, but he laughs it off now, saying, "The bureaucracy was involved." The region, historically known as Graves de Bordeaux, lies to the south of the Médoc and southeast of the city of Bordeaux. Currently the region has sixty-eight châteaux, including some of the most prestigious, the foremost being Château Haut-Brion. Samuel Pepys wrote of the wines of "ho bryan" in his diary in 1663, and Thomas Jefferson so enjoyed them that he brought 125 bottles home with him to America. It later became the only property in the 1855 classification for red wines that was outside the Médoc—and as a first growth, no less. And it is still going strong, with the 2005 wine receiving some critics' highest marks of the vintage. Château Pape-Clement, also in the region, has made seven hundred vintages of wine, starting on a vineyard owned by the archbishop of Bordeaux who later became Pope Clement V. The property has catapulted to greater recognition under its current owner, Bernard Magrez. Château Smith Haut Lafitte makes some acclaimed dry white wines, as does Lurton's La Louvière.

Nevertheless, the region has suffered from an image problem. Lurton says that in part it had to do with the fact that Graves, which means "gravels" in French and refers to the gravelly topsoil, was not an uplifting name in English. Also, the wines from the south of Graves were not held in as high repute. So Lurton spearheaded a movement to change the name and organized a group of several dozen growers into a *syndicat de defense,* or syndicate. They sought to change the name to Northern Graves, but, under European law, duplication of an existing appellation name is not allowed, even with a qualifier such as "Northern." So the group settled on the name of Pessac-Léognan, after the two main towns in the region. Their application, formally filed in 1980, had to illustrate the distinctive history of the region and make a case for its recognition, as well as show climatic differences from the rump Graves appellation. Objections from the growers in the south caused additional delays. But the application eventually made its way out of the regional committee of the INAO to the national committee, which then had an independent commission review the application and the *terroir* itself.

The producers' request was formally approved on September 9, 1987, granting the producers the ability to set their own production norms within the newly established zone. The Pessac-Léognan appellation includes 3,800 acres of vineyards in ten towns. The regulations of

TABLE I. COMPARATIVE APPELLATION
CONTROLS

	Pessac-Léognan	Médoc	Bordeaux
Area (hectares)	1,600	4,500	60,561
Varieties	Cabernet Sauvignon	Cabernet Sauvignon	Cabernet Sauvignon
	Cabernet Franc	Cabernet Franc	Cabernet Franc
	Carmenère	Carmenère	Carmenère
	Malbec	Malbec	Malbec
	Merlot	Merlot	Merlot
	Petit Verdot	Petit Verdot	Petit Verdot
	Whites:		Whites:
	Sémillon		Sémillon
	Sauvignon Blanc		Sauvignon Blanc
	Muscadelle		Muscadelle
Minimum vine density	6,500 vines/hectare	6,500–10,000 vines/hectare	No restriction
Base yield (hectoliters/ hectare)	45	50	55 (red) 65 (white)
Minimum natural sugars (grams/liter)	178	170	178
Minimum alcohol level (%)	10.5	10	10.5
Tasting by committee	Obligatory for quality certificate	Obligatory for quality certificate	Obligatory for quality certificate

SOURCE: Comparison of AOC *décrets*.

the appellation have the power of law over various aspects of production. All the grapes must be grown within the appellation's boundaries, and the yields must be kept low. To make red wine, château owners can grow only six red-grape varieties, including the well-known Cabernet Sauvignon and Merlot and a supporting cast of lesser-known grapes. They must harvest by a certain date and achieve a certain minimum level of natural sugar in the grapes and alcohol in the wine. The final wine must be a blend, and it must bear the name of the appellation on the label. Similar controls are in effect in the 470 appellations throughout France (see table I).

WHAT IS *TERROIR?*

The concept of *terroir* underpins the appellation system in France. One of those frustratingly difficult words to translate, it has been defined by Jay McInerney as "location, location, location." Essentially it means the growing area, starting with the soil *(la terre)* and the slope, and taking into account other elements of the vineyard's microclimate, such as sun, rain, wind, and temperature fluctuations. Each *terroir* produces a unique wine, according to the partisans of *terroir*, sometimes whimsically called *terroirists.* Even if two vineyards (or even vineyard parcels) in Burgundy both grow Pinot Noir, or two vineyards in Bordeaux grow Cabernet Sauvignon, the wines they produce will likely always differ because of the *terroir.* The appellation system seeks to promote and protect these local variations. Appellation wines are labeled according to the growing area instead of the grape variety.

Some critics who dispute the importance of *terroir* argue that decisions made by the vineyard manager or winemaker are more important than the soil and climate. Are the vines thinned early in the season or late? Is the vineyard irrigated? What type of oak is used in winemaking—new barrels, American oak, oak chips, or none at all? The appellation rules dictate standards for many of these human factors as well, in the effort to maintain a regional style.

A final requirement little known among consumers is that the appellation wines must be tasted by a committee consisting of producers, merchants, INAO agents, and perhaps a critic. The goal of these blind tastings is to ensure consistency from one year to the next. The wine must also have a certain local or regional character, known as *typicité*. This regional specificity justifies the entire territorially based system. Even an excellent wine can theoretically be rejected if it is not considered representative. Because these tastings generally occur before December of the harvest year, many of the big red wines are tasted while they are still extremely young. If the wine fails to meet the criteria of the appellation, it is "declassified," or downgraded to *vin de table* (see table 2). However, these tasting committees have become toothless in recent years, as almost all wines pass.

The small appellations such as Pessac-Léognan are restrictive. St.-Julien, St.-Estèphe, and Margaux are more so, as their growing zones are smaller and official yields slightly lower. But one château can produce wine from multiple appellations, even on the same property. An example is Château d'Issan in Margaux (figure 1). To the left of the long

TABLE 2. THREE CATEGORIES
OF FRENCH WINES

Appellation d'origine contrôlée (AOC)	*Vin de pays*	*Vin de table*
Accounts for more than half the volume of French wine production and more than three-quarters of all sales. All of the top wines from France are from the 475 appellations. The category is popular with producers, who rarely leave an appellation once they join.	The category, created in 1983, allows the listing of grape varieties on the label, but no blending is allowed. It has grown to account for a quarter of French wine production. Much *vin de pays* is exported.	A declining category, *vin de table* wines are the most frequently sent for distillation. If an appellation wine is rejected, then it falls to the *vin de table* category. No vintages, place names, or grape varieties can be specified on the labels of *vin de table*.

driveway, flanked by tall trees, that leads to the moat-encircled château lies the vineyard that produces the top wine. But to the right lies another vineyard that is classified AOC Bordeaux Supérieur. Emmanuel Cruse, the general manager, explained to me that the vineyard on the right used to be used for grazing sheep. Planted only in 1984, the vineyard was about thirty years too late to be classified as Margaux, as a moratorium on growth of the appellation went into effect in 1955. Thus an AOC Bordeaux Supérieur vineyard lies directly adjacent to an AOC Margaux vineyard. The soil is slightly heavier, but the real reason for the distinction is politics. Cruse is optimistic that in the next few years, the appellation will be allowed to expand again, and all his property will be classified as Margaux. But the wheels of the bureaucracy turn slowly.

A château often determines its own quality controls, which may be stricter than those of the AOC, and, with all the wine available that meets the AOC standards, the winemakers can create a flagship label with the best wine and a "second" label with less good wine. The volume produced of the second wine often varies. Top producers may send as little as 35 percent of the harvest to the top wine and the rest to the second wine. How closely the second wine resembles the *grand vin* varies by producer.

Commentators, consumers, and others without a stake in the *appellation* system occasionally accuse the producers of being insensitive to demand, in large part because of their efforts to maintain *typicité*.

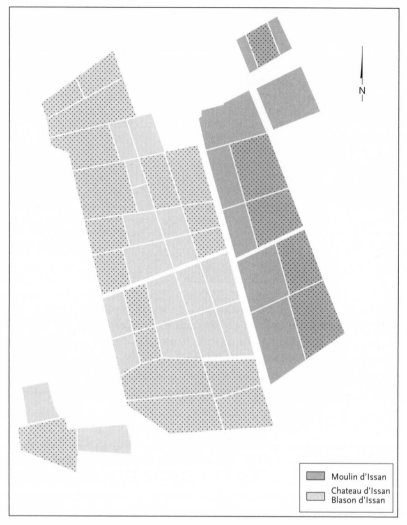

Figure 1. A tale of two vineyards: Château d'Issan, Margaux. Because they were added to the château's holdings too late to qualify for the Margaux appellation, the vineyards on the east side of the driveway are classified as the less prestigious AOC Bordeaux Supérieur.

That's true. There is probably not one Syrah or Chardonnay vine planted in Bordeaux. Because these varieties have not been traditionally grown in Bordeaux, no syndicate will permit them. The rationale is the risk of failure if the new variety did not take well to the soil. But the larger risk is that introducing an extremely popular variety would place the wines of Bordeaux in more direct competition with wines from elsewhere in the world, unleashing competition on the basis of price rather than *terroir*. Thus the producers have opted for stability and tradition. But the system is not working for red wines, as the practice of crisis distillation has shown, and customers appear to not be fans of Bordeaux whites. In 1979, 35 percent of the vineyards of Bordeaux grew white-wine varieties; by 1999, Sauvignon Blanc, Semillon, and the other permitted white-wine grapes accounted for only 15 percent of the total area planted. A winemaker who seeks to experiment, even with the intent of fully expressing the *terroir*, risks declassification if he or she strays too far from the traditional style. Nicolas Joly, who makes a very successful wine from Chenin Blanc grapes in the Loire, told me that his wines, which are natural yet distinctive, often encounter criticism during the blind tasting in the syndicate.

→>—<←

Many appellations place limits on the yield of fruit per hectare of vines in the name of maintaining quality, but a constant increase in yields has only exacerbated the crisis in the region. "France is a nation of rules and of rule breakers," writes one notable critic when discussing yields.[5] The basis of the limits is the prevailing viticultural wisdom that lower yields produce better wine. [6] The theory is, roughly, that if the grower thins buds and shoots from the vine early in the season, or prunes some of the crop as the fruit is developing, the remaining fruit will have higher sugar levels, which yield more intense flavor and a higher alcohol content.[7] Moreover, poor soil tends to produce better grapes.[8]

Yield is one area where economic logic seems to support viticultural practice, as reduced supply creates scarcity value. The "base yields" of the fifty-seven appellations in Bordeaux express this relationship. High-end appellations set their base yields (for unfermented juice) at 45 hectoliters per hectare (hL/ha), and the most diluted AOC Bordeaux sets the yield at 55 hL/ha. For white wines, the base yields are even higher, at 65 hL/ha. Beyond Bordeaux, the national wine authority, Viniflhor, sets the national maximum yield for the lower grades of wine: 80 hL/ha for *vin de pays* and 90 hL/ha for table wines. Yields in the Charentes region have a special exemption to use a base yield of 130 hL/ha because almost all of that fruit is used to make cognac, for which the distillation process reduces the volume dramatically.

Even this economic logic has come into question, however. Yields in Bordeaux have been rising over time. For several decades around 1800,

Château Latour had yields of 12 hL/ha.[9] In the 1950s, the average yield in Bordeaux was around 30 hL/ha, and in the 1960s it rose to 40 hL/ha. But the sharpest increase has come since 1970, when the average yield was 30 hL/ha: in the period 1995–99, the average annual yield was 58 hL/ha.[10] Wine reviews of these years were, on the whole, favorable, and the prices also rose sharply. Excellent years for quality, particularly 1982 and 1986, have also produced high quantities. Thus low yields are not in and of themselves a reliable indicator of high quality in Bordeaux.

The recent rise in yields is due in large part to a 1974 change in INAO legislation. The reform meant that in all AOCs, the stated yields would simply serve as a guideline from which the producers' actual yields would be allowed to diverge within a 40 percent range. However, the rule is slightly disingenuous, because the producer syndicates almost invariably request a higher yield limit, not a lower one. This upper limit is called the *plafond limite de classement* ("ceiling limit," abbreviated as PLC). Every year by November 25, the syndicate must send a harvest declaration to the INAO that gives the dates of harvest, total crop, and yields. The syndicate can request permission—particularly in good years—to increase the yields above the normal yield and right up to the ceiling limit. Because of the close relationship between producers and the INAO staff, the organization almost always approves these requests. In 1983, another reform raised the base yields from 40 to 45 hL/ha across all AOCs in the Bordeaux region. This change benefited the smallest appellations of the Médoc the most, permitting them a 12.5 percent increase. The ceiling limit was also raised, allowing a higher yield overall.

The system founders when production levels significantly or consistently exceed the base yield. The productive potential of the Médoc vineyards easily surpasses 45 to 50 hL/ha. In 1990, the average yield in AOC Médoc was 87 hL/ha. This was an unusually abundant year, but several growers admit that high vine density can easily lead to yields of 60 to 70 hL/ha.[11] In this situation, the claim of an inverse relation between yield and quality breaks down. Under the system in effect between 1935 and 1983, when a grower's yield exceeded the base yield, the wine would "cascade" into the lower, less prestigious AOC: the excess in the small appellations would go to AOC Médoc, the AOC Médoc excess would go to AOC Bordeaux, and AOC Bordeaux excess would go to the distillery. Since 1983, the château has been required to submit the entire crop to one AOC. If it is rejected, then it is classified as *vin de table*. Thus, in theory, the producers must manage their yields to hit the yield ceiling exactly or risk the rejection of their whole production. In practice, a first rejection

CAN CARS RUN ON CABERNET?

When French winemakers cannot sell their wine, the state guarantees a minimum price for distillation. Under the Common Agricultural Policy, the EU contributes some aid for "crisis" distillations (€3.30 per degree of alcohol per one hundred liters), and member states can match but not exceed this amount. Distillation has been most important for the Languedoc, a longtime bastion of bulk wine that is now experiencing a dynamic transition to quality. But in 2005, for the first time, a glut of appellation wine could not be sold, and 1.08 billion liters (122 million nine-liter cases) went to the distillery. Kermit Lynch, an American importer of fine French wine, told me, "It was really awful stuff."

This excess wine is distilled and reduced to almost pure ethanol, which then becomes a fuel additive. Whether the process is energy-efficient remains a matter of debate: some critics point out that the net energy yielded from such biofuel is low or even negative, and others note that ethanol produces a higher level of carbon dioxide emissions than regular gasoline. Either way, however, it keeps jobs in the industry that provides the raw material, whether corn in America or grapes in the European Union. And running your car on Cabernet at least sounds better than running it on corn.

---

leads to another review, and violations of yields have to be "really flagrant" for the syndicates and the INAO to take action.[12]

Frequent changes in yield limits suggest that the real purpose of the policy is economic management rather than quality control. And, given that much AOC wine is now consigned to the distillery, it is not working well for that purpose, either. A telling characteristic is that the date for setting the yield is about ten weeks *after* the start of the harvest. This gives the producer and the *négociant* sufficient time to check stock levels, track import and export levels, and perform market studies. Of course, a downward adjustment of the base limit might be needed if bad weather spoiled the harvest, but it is hard to see a viticultural justification for adjusting the limit upward. As one national trade association director told me, "The system has been perverted. With this (AOC) system, we do economic management. That's fine. But you have to call a spade a spade!"[13]

Occasionally the yield ceiling is so stretched as to make a mockery of the official limit. In the 1999 vintage from Burgundy, yields were allowed to float as high as 40 percent above the level stated in the syndicate's founding documents.[14] Actual production yields may have been as much as double the base yield. What is a winegrower to do with so

GRAND VIN DE BORDEAUX

2002

CHÂTEAU

LA LOUVIÈRE

PESSAC-LÉOGNAN

APPELLATION PESSAC-LÉOGNAN CONTRÔLÉE

GRAVES

SCEA LES VIGNOBLES

ANDRÉ LURTON

VITICULTEUR À LÉOGNAN

GIRONDE - FRANCE

MIS EN BOUTEILLE AU CHATEAU

PRODUCE OF FRANCE

PRODUCT OF FRANCE   BORDEAUX TABLE WINE

IMPORTED BY:

W.J. DEUTSCH & SONS LTD, HARRISON, N.Y.

ALC. 13% BY VOL.   750 ML

much wine? The excess has four outlets: the so-called *cave secrète*, where undeclared wines can be sold on the premises for cash; the "cascade," in which all the excess of one classification category is classified at the next level down; the practice of "bleeding" juice from the grape must, leaving behind a more concentrated product; and distillation, an option that carries a certain stigma and fetches a low price. Because such practices are employed well after the harvest, the harvest report might still claim that the grower managed to hit the yield limit exactly. However, there are limits to how far the rules can be bent. In vintage year 2000 in Burgundy, INAO refused to allow another 40 percent increase in the PLC. In the 2001 growing season, INAO agents performed more checks to ensure that growers were pruning sufficiently.[15] Given the current overproduction, the organization is making more of an effort to hold the line on yield increases and use them as originally intended, to limit the quantity of wine on the market and raise quality.

THE POLITICS OF A BORDEAUX LABEL

MANDATORY ITEMS

1   *Appellation d'origine contrôlée:* This item certifies that 100 percent of the grapes used in the wine come from the specified growing area and that the wine meets all of the production standards—set by the producers themselves—for the appellation.

2   Volume of the wine: 75 centiliters (750 milliliters) is standard; other bottle sizes are available.

3   Alcohol by volume: Must be the exact percentage.

4   Control number or lot identification number (may appear on capsule).

5   *Mis en bouteille à la propriété:* Indicates that the wine was bottled on the wine-grower's property. The inclusion of this specification resulted from scandals among *négociants,* which made estate bottling a sign of quality and a source of greater profits for the château.

6   Country of origin: Must be indicated for all export wine.

7   Since 2000, the term *vin de Bordeaux* or *grand vin de Bordeaux* (to designate higher-quality wines) has been included.

OPTIONAL ITEMS

8   Name of the producer.

9   Vintage: Certifies that 100 percent of the grapes were harvested in the year shown on the label.

10 Label art, which usually depicts the château.

For the top wines of the region, often but not always removed from the issue of yields, growers have other ways to prop up prices through what is known as the *place de Bordeaux,* a marketplace where producers sell to *négociants.* First, producers sell future vintages about eighteen to twenty-four months before they are shipped to retailers. Thus they are not only paid two years before the wine is delivered—great payment terms in any business—but also enjoy price protection in the event that wines from a given vintage sell for less when they are ultimately released (which could happen because of macroeconomic variables, a change in critical reception of a vintage once it is in the bottle, or a subsequent vintage's attracting more interest). Recently, however, this practice has favored the buyer, as prices have risen tremendously in the interim period.[16] Second, the Bordeaux châteaux sell their new wines in multiple *tranches* (releases). In the nineteenth century, there were only two *tranches,* and the first was always larger.[17] In recent highly touted vintages, however, the producers have released only a small quantity in the first *tranche,* creating an "intentional manipulation."[18] The second *tranche* included only another small quantity. By the time they released the third *tranche,* the prices were 50 to 100 percent above the original price. Some châteaux even use a fourth *tranche.* Third, the most prestigious houses often tie sales of their top wine (*grand vin*) to sales of multiple cases of the second wine or other labels in the portfolio. This commercial savoir-faire supports the view of one British retailer that "the Bordelais are merchants and businessmen, not farmers. Burgundy is the other way around."[19]

THE SHIFTING BALANCE OF POWER BETWEEN CHÂTEAUX AND NÉGOCIANTS

The château owners and the *négociants,* or merchants, have competed for profits and argued over quality for the past 150 years. In sharp contrast to the situation in the United States, where the separation between winemakers and distributors was legally mandated after Prohibition, in France the division between the two groups is maintained not by law but by the historical structure of the wine trade. The balance of power has long favored the *négociants.* Not only do they store and sell wine, but they have also played a role in blending it. In the early days of Bordeaux winemaking, they exported the wine around Europe. Thus the winegrowing region came to be known as Bordeaux, the name of the city where the merchants were located, rather than as the growing area of the Gironde. Most other top wine areas in France, such as Champagne and Burgundy, are named after growing areas, not cities in them; only the merchants of Porto had similar clout. The producers regained name recognition and thus power after the 1855 classification. In 1920, Château Mouton Rothschild became the first château to bring production and bottling onto the property. This trend accelerated in the 1970s, swinging power back to the château proprietors.

Over a ten-year period beginning in the early 1970s, the Bordeaux wine industry followed a condensed version of late-nineteenth-century French viticulture: boom, bust, scandal, and new institutions. The high quality and low quantity of the 1971 vintage pushed prices to unprecedented levels. Consumers and the industry were thirsty for a good year. The 1968 vintage had been a "small, disastrous crop in terms of quality and quantity," according to Robert Parker, and although quantities rose in 1969, the vintage was still what Parker called (with the benefit of hindsight) "my candidate for the most undesirable wines produced in Bordeaux in the last 30 years."[20] The press vigorously promoted the promise of the 1971 vintage: *Le Monde* ran a story under the headline "The Stampede to Red Gold," *Le Figaro* had a page-one story titled "Bordeaux: The Return of the Golden Age," the weekly *L'Express* featured a story on "Gold in the Bottles," and *Le Monde de l'Économie* ran the headline "Fever in the Vineyard." The regional newspaper *Sud-Ouest* focused on the high demand with its story "The Black Market and Red Bordeaux." Philippe Roudie claims that "no one in France could ignore what was happening in the Gironde."[21] This attention drove up the prices again for the 1972 vintage, which turned out to be mediocre. Edmund Penning-Rowsell charts the rise in price of one *tonneau* (900 liters) of Château Talbot from 1969 to 1972: 10,000 francs, 12,000 francs, 31,000 francs, and 55,000 francs respectively.[22]

International factors also contributed to the boom. First, the demand from overseas escalated sharply. The United States almost doubled imports of Bordeaux wine in four years, from 70,000 hL in 1969 to 130,000 hL in 1972. The Japanese also developed a taste for Bordeaux, and Japan rose from the thirteenth to the fourth biggest importer between 1969 and 1972. Second, foreign investors were eager to reap a share of the wealth: capital flowed in, and foreign firms bought up winegrowing properties.

In 1973 the speculative bubble burst. Worldwide recession sapped demand, and prices started to collapse, particularly for low-end wines. A rift developed between growers and local *négociants,* as it had at the beginning of the century. Both groups had representatives on the Conseil Interprofessionnel des Vins de Bordeaux (CIVB), or Bordeaux Wine Council, which undertook common promotional activities and market studies. Blaming the price decline on the *négociants,* growers resigned from the CIVB en masse in July 1974, and stayed away despite pleas from as high up as the Ministry of Agriculture. This left a rump of *négociants* and regional officials. In sharp contrast to the newspaper stories of two years prior, articles now talked about the "problem of wine" and proposed delaying the tax payments of small producers.

Meanwhile, the growers were becoming more agitated. In February 1974 they demonstrated in downtown Bordeaux, and small-scale demonstrations continued all over the region. In April 1975 their actions became more destructive: growers blocked the A10 highway to

Paris and the Bordeaux-Marseilles train line, dumping 320,000 liters of wine at various train stations. In April 1975, 1,400 vines were uprooted from the property of the *négociant* Richard. Another 3,000 vines were uprooted in St. Léon at the property of the Bordeaux *négociant* Castel Pières; this incident was followed by a "visit of the vandals" to another Castel property. In March 1976, violence against the *négociants* restarted in Blayais, where as many as 20,000 vines were destroyed at one property.[23]

Even more damaging to the Bordeaux wine industry than the weakening global economy was a winemaking scandal involving the *négociants*.[24] At its center was the prestigious Cruse firm, one of the leading exporting *négociants* and one of the most patrician and respected merchant families. The brains behind the operation was Pierre Bert, who bought AOC Bordeaux white wine and red table wine from outside Bordeaux and switched the paperwork, selling the red as AOC Bordeaux and pocketing a significant markup. Tried in December 1974, Bert went to prison for one year and was heavily fined. Two members of the Cruse family were also found guilty, although they received suspended sentences.

As the scandal unfolded in late 1973, it became entangled with national politics. Two cabinet members, Valéry Giscard d'Estaing and Jacques Chaban-Delmas, known as the "duke of Aquitaine," were vying to succeed the ailing president, Georges Pompidou.[25] The hard-hitting satirical newspaper *Le Canard Enchaîné* broke the scandal with the page-one headline "All-Out Fraud in Bordeaux" and linked it to the national political drama with the headline "Bordeaux Wine: Giscard Sees Red." Because some families among the *négociants* had long been key supporters of Chaban-Delmas, the story concluded: "Another point for Giscard! Poor Jacques!" The story was picked up by all the other papers, national to local, right to left. They called it Winegate, and it effectively ended the presidential hopes of Chaban-Delmas.[26]

The scandal was also the last straw for the Bordeaux growers and *négociants*. Prices tumbled across the region, and exports slowed. American demand dropped back to 1969 levels and stayed there until the excellent 1982 vintage. A series of other minor scandals, involving watering down wine, called into question the integrity of the entire Bordeaux wine industry; however, because the scandals were more damaging to the *négociants*, they turned the tables in favor of the château proprietors.

Some châteaux stopped dealing with the *négociants*. Small châteaux across the region started using direct sales to reach the domestic market.

The need to reduce stock was so urgent and the power of the merchants so limited that in June 1975 Lafite and Mouton Rothschild bypassed the merchants completely and jointly sold six thousand cases of their wines at Christie's auction house.[27] Some foreign buyers even began going straight to the château, skipping the *négociants*.

Perhaps the most lasting change in the relationship between proprietors and merchants was new importance of the phrase *mis en bouteille au château* ("bottled at the château," suggesting a minimum of *négociant* involvement). The scandals led the châteaux to wash their hands of the *négociants* by bringing production in-house. Not only did this designation suggest higher quality, but the practice wrested control of winemaking and bottling, with their the high added value, away from the *négociants*.

This shift was, however, a largely symbolic victory for the proprietors, as many of the châteaux lacked the technical knowledge and the capital for in-house winemaking and bottling. Their solution was to bring the *négociants* in-house to do the production. This way *mis en bouteille* could still appear on the label, but the owners could benefit from the *négociants'* expertise. This practice continues, as a busy group of mobile winemakers drive their production vans from château to château to make and bottle wine on the premises.

In the mid-1970s, fresh capital and institutional reform restored the status of the merchants. Many of the top *négociant* houses sold out to big foreign firms such as Bass, Seagram's, and Allied Breweries.[28] These firms provided capital and marketing clout. The CIVB was reconstituted and reformed in February 1976, signaling an end to the hostilities between growers and *négociants* and recognition of their intertwined fates. The new CIVB maintains parity between members from the two "families" of production and *négociants*. The presidency alternates between the two groups, and decisions are reached by consensus. The CIVB remains an important body for bridging the divide between the two groups. In 2005, its €21 million budget, derived from a levy on the members of the trade, funded economic, marketing, and technical activities.

In the 1990s the two "families" of Bordeaux wine reached a delicate truce, and since then the rising tide of a string of good vintages has buoyed relations. A scandal in 1998 somewhat tarnished the proprietors' collective reputation; meanwhile, two changes have boosted the position of the merchants. First, the line between producers and *négociants* has begun to blur. For example, the firm Baron Philippe de

Rothschild, S.A., is now not only the holding company for Château Mouton Rothschild and several other high-end producers but also a large *négociant* house. It distributes domestic production of affiliated companies' wine. Each side of the sector is also consolidating.[29] There were 35,000 declared growers in Bordeaux in 1970, 12,500 in 1999, and 10,000 in 2005. The average area each grower owns and maintains has increased from 2.5 hectares to almost 10 hectares.[30] Among the *négociants,* the top 30 firms are now doing 85 percent of the business.[31] Second, the *négociants* favor brands, such as Mouton Cadet (Baron Rothschild) or Sirius (Sichel), and brands now dominate the global wine trade. The scandal that led to the popularity of estate bottling may, however, still limit the power of brands, as it perpetuates the practice (however economically inefficient it may be) of bottling on the property and not at the *négociant* house.

Today, it seems that the proprietor-merchant divide is being replaced by a quality divide. The leading two hundred châteaux have had little difficulty selling their wines in recent vintages, and their owners now include some of the biggest names in French business, such as LVMH, AXA, and Bouygues. Their wines, which now command stratospheric prices on release, have become accoutrements of the global elite, along with sports cars and silk scarves. As demand outstrips supply, the prices continue to rise. At an international trade show in 2004, Robert Parker said that he expected prices for the collectible wines of the 2005 vintage to continue to rise, as increasing demand among the newly wealthy of the developing world met static supply from the leading châteaux. "Château Lynches Bages," he said, gesturing at fellow panelist Jean-Michel Cazes, the owner of the château, "will always produce the same number of cases."[32]

But, moving down the quality scale, the thousands of smallholders in far-flung areas have had either a hard time or a very hard time. These growers are angry and dissatisfied. Their frustration, as in the 1970s, has sometimes taken the form of destructive acts, such as bricking up the doors to the CIVB building one night in December 2005, heaping manure on the doorstep of a *négociant* a month later, and ripping up vines at André Lurton's Château Bonnet in Entre-Deux-Mers. Small growers are retiring or quitting at the rate of three hundred a year in Bordeaux alone.

The large grower syndicate that controls Bordeaux and Bordeaux Supérieur briefly took the law of supply and demand into its own hands. Given the weak price (€700) for a 900-liter *tonneau,* the growers voted in December 2005 to withhold the appellation seal from any wine that was sold to a *négociant* for less than €1,000. After months of sluggish sales, however, they relaxed the rule.

That will bring some of their wines to the distillery door. In 2005, 18 million liters of wine were distilled in Bordeaux alone. In all of France, more than 1 billion liters of appellation wine were distilled. However, these quantities were well under the authorized distillation ceilings of 50 million liters in Bordeaux and 1.5 billion liters nationally, indicating that growers were not offering as much wine for distillation as policy makers had hoped. The 2006 level was raised to 4 billion liters.

Roland Feredj, the executive director of the CIVB, would prefer to combat the problem of oversupply at the root—literally. He favors eliminating public funds—both European and domestic—for distillation and offering a premium for uprooting vines, then letting the producers take the consequences. "If a winemaker takes a premium for ripping up vines and then can't sell his wine—too bad. You have to make people responsible. On an open and liberal market, you need to find your niche in the market." In February 2005, the CIVB effectively doubled the premium for uprooting vines, bringing it from the European level of €6,300 per hectare (2.47 acres) to €12,000. About 1,800 hectares of vines, equivalent to about 1.5 percent of the region's vineyards, were uprooted in 2005.[33]

Bordeaux is certainly not the only part of France experiencing difficulty; indeed, other areas are suffering more. In the Mâcon in Burgundy, riot police used tear gas to break up demonstrations in September 2005. In the Languedoc, where overproduction is the most acute because of the huge vineyard area, growers have turned to violence. A group of *vignerons* calling themselves the Comité Régional d'Action Viticole (CRAV) have started a campaign of vandalism to call attention to their plight. In one night in March 2005, they shut down eighty miles of train tracks, set three freight cars on fire, and destroyed a switching station. They took sledgehammers to thirteen tanks of Chilean wine at a distillery and let one million liters flow into the streets. They later blew up a tanker truck of Spanish wine (the driver escaped unharmed), staged a rolling roadblock on the A9 highway and clashed with police, bombed a tax collector's office and a call center (there were no injuries), and attacked the local facility of a top Bordeaux *négociant*. Jean Huillet, the head of the Hérault wine cooperative, attacked the "growing wealth of the *négociants* . . . [and

the] supermarkets, which, for the most part, are shamelessly stran-
gling us."[34]

-+>-<+-

If rule-bending and flexible relations have helped keep the appellation
system alive, what factors turned it into a potential disaster? A main
cause has been sluggish or declining exports in a market where French
wines must now compete with reliable and low-cost wines from regions
such as Australia, Chile, and Argentina. (See chapter 5.) At home, the
French wine industry, like that in the United States decades ago, has
faced increasing social and political opposition to drinking that has
contributed to a long-term decline in per capita consumption. Such
measures as the tightening of advertising laws and a campaign against
drunk driving arguably are beyond the industry's control. However,
another cause of the current crisis is of the industry's own making: institutional bloat, which has exacerbated regional rivalries and heightened
the perception that rules are being imposed from the outside.

The Rise of Resistance

Claude Évin was first elected to the National Assembly in 1978 at the
age of twenty-eight and has served in it ever since. Born in the Loire
region, he studied law and has also served as mayor on and off in the
town of Saint-Nazaire in his home district. As health minister in 1990,
he brought about the passage of a bill that mandated separate smoking
and nonsmoking sections in restaurants and had far-reaching effects on
the advertising of tobacco and alcohol. The law, known officially as
number 91–32, to "fight against tobacco and alcohol abuse," has
become known simply as the Évin law.[35]

The Évin law was the first strike in a series of antialcohol campaigns
that have threatened the privileged position of wine in French culture.[36] The law severely restricted not only direct advertisements for
tobacco and alcohol in print and on television but also "indirect"
advertisements, such as the placement of product names at sporting
events, on soccer players' jerseys, billboards, or Formula 1 race cars.[37]
A requirement that print advertisements for both tobacco and alcohol
must carry a warning about the dangers of excessive consumption
enraged wine industry participants, especially as evidence was simulta-
neously emerging that attested to the health benefits of the moderate
consumption of red wine.

As the campaigns against alcohol escalated, wine was frequently lumped unceremoniously with spirits, a conflation that ignored the traditional distinction between *l'alcool* and *les alcools* and the special place of wine in French culture. Many antialcohol campaigns from the Ministry of Health represent daily alcohol consumption levels as glasses of wine, irking members of the wine trade. In one report, alcohol was placed in the same category ("very dangerous") as heroin and cocaine; in another, wine producers were outraged to learn, the treatment recommended for alcoholics was the same as that for drug addicts. Another report proposed a national "day without alcohol" modeled on the "day without tobacco"; and yet another recommended taxing wine in proportion to its alcohol content.[38] The Ministry of Education also started a campaign against excessive teen drinking.[39]

The wine sector has strongly objected to being made the scapegoat for alcoholism.[40] The president of the National Committee on AOC wines commented at their general assembly in 1999: "The quality growers are completely fed up with the multiple accusations leveled at wine products. The laws seek to conflate wine with other alcoholic products, even though numerous scientific studies recognize a specificity of wine."[41] Other advocates underscore the social cohesiveness that stems from drinking wine: "Drinking is a social act, so in our view, when they try to stamp out a glass of wine, they are stamping out a way of life."[42] In response to the perceived threat presented by the Évin law, various associations (mostly producer groups) in the wine sector formed the Association for Wine and Society in 1995. The major firms in the drinks industry, particularly wine *négociants,* have formed the group Entreprises et Prévention (Business and Prevention) to at least appear willing partners in the campaign to encourage responsible consumption.[43]

The stringent restrictions on advertising have hurt wine producers. The Évin law prohibited television advertising, and all print and billboard ads had to carry a warning: "Abuse of alcohol is dangerous for your health. Consume it in moderation." Further restrictions prohibited the use of models and seductive poses and limited wording to technical, nonsubjective information (see figure 2). Pictures of people enjoying wine with meals were banned. Billboards were limited in size and prohibited in cities. Posters were also banned, except for producers' logos on things such as café umbrellas.

French laws against drunk driving have also been strengthened in the past decade in an effort to reduce the road fatality rate, which was

Figure 2. Advertising restrictions in France. Which one of these publicity photos of the winemaker Catherine Gachet was allowed under the Évin law? (Hint: no sultry looks allowed.) Gachet, who owns a château in the Barsac appellation of Bordeaux, could pose for the Bordeaux wine campaign only because she is in the trade: the law prohibits the use of models. Images courtesy CIVB.

Catherine,
viticultrice à Sauternes.

Toutes ces Appellations font partie des Vins d'Or de Bordeaux

Sauternes
Barsac
Loupiac
Cadillac
Sainte-Croix-du-Mont
Cérons

SAUTERNES
BORDEAUX
tout un monde de finesse

Graves Supérieures
Bordeaux Supérieur
Côtes de Bordeaux-St Macaire
Premières Côtes de Bordeaux
Ste-Foy-Bordeaux

www.vins-bordeaux.fr

L'ABUS D'ALCOOL EST DANGEREUX POUR LA SANTÉ. A CONSOMMER AVEC MODÉRATION.

above the EU average. Jacques Chirac made road safety a campaign issue in the 2002 presidential election, and the Ministry of Transportation introduced several measures to increase public awareness and enforce existing laws. Wine producers and rural restaurateurs have inveighed bitterly against the campaign, arguing that the laws are cutting into restaurant profits by reducing the on-premises consumption of alcohol. Sales of sweet wines in France, which have been in decline for decades, have fallen precipitously under the new policy regime, as many diners now forgo after-dinner drinks. Some restaurateurs now offer doggie bags so that diners will continue to order wine with their meals and take the unused portion home with them. These efforts have apparently succeeded: although the road fatalities in all advanced industrial democracies have declined, thanks to advances in car safety and crackdowns on drunk driving, France's has dropped dramatically: the road fatality rate fell from 157 per million inhabitants in 1994 to 93 per million in 2004, below the EU average of 95 per million.

Against this backdrop, it is small wonder that the consumption of wine has been declining (see table 3). After World War II, per capita consumption returned to the early-twentieth-century peak of one hundred liters per year. But then it started to decline as lunch breaks shortened, consumers opted for other drinks (such as beer, mineral water, or soda), and the

TABLE 3. FRENCH WINE CONSUMPTION PER CAPITA,
1960–2004 (LITERS)

1960	1990	1995	2000	2004
100	72.56	62.94	58.18	54.77

SOURCE: Data for 1960 from Onivins; data for 1990–2004 from *The U.S. Wine Market: Impact Databank, Review, and Forecast* (New York: M. Shanken Communications, 2005).

antialcohol campaigns kicked in. Although declines have also occurred in other wine-producing countries with high rates of per capita consumption, France has seen the sharpest drop.[44] But even as overall consumption is declining, the quality is rising: French consumers are apparently drinking less but better wine. As one senior official told me in Paris, *vin de table* or *vin ordinaire*, the cheapest wine, is "the wine of grandparents."[45] Indeed, the *Economist* summed up the shrinking low end by saying, "There's no call for *ordinaire*."[46] But as the demand for quality wine has risen, it has become more important to certify that quality. The appellation system, now extended to include many new wine regions as well as to cover other beverages and foodstuffs, is critically overburdened.

+>-<+

The Institut National des Appellations d'Origine (INAO) is a parapublic entity. Its founding in 1935, after twenty years of negotiations and incremental steps, highlighted the importance of the wine sector in France: wine was virtually the only agricultural product to warrant its own governing institutions. The INAO facilitated the development and implementation of wine policy, emphasizing the importance of industry self-governance. The wine *professionels* have always held sway in policymaking, with the *syndicat* serving a key role at the base of the organizational pyramid.

The purpose of the INAO, with its Paris headquarters and twenty-six regional offices, is to link distinctive, high-quality products with the geographic location where they are made. Thus *terroir* is at the heart of the INAO. Appellation wines are important French exports, as they have a top spot in net agricultural trade. But two changes intended to exploit this advantage have made INAO a victim of its own success.

The first major change has been the expansion of AOCs for wine. In 1950, AOCs accounted for 12 percent of the winegrowing area of France.[47] By 1970, they had expanded to around 20 percent; by 2004, they covered 54 percent of the territory under vine in France, or 450,000 hectares, and accounted for 46 percent of the volume of wine produced.[48]

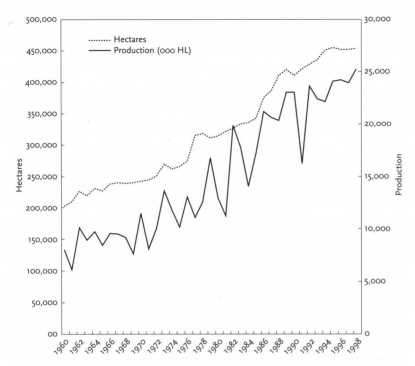

Figure 3. Growth in appellation wines, 1960–98. Data from INAO.

Figure 3 charts this expansion. At the same time, the total area under vine in France declined, from about 1.2 million hectares in 1970 to 830,000 in 1998.[49] In Bordeaux, as recently as 1983, only three-quarters of the vineyards were AOC.[50] By 1999, 99 percent of the vineyards, or 115,000 hectares, were AOC. However, as the quantity of appellation wine has increased, quality has not necessarily kept pace. The rejection of substandard wines in the marketplace rather than in the AOC *syndicat* has meant that more appellation wines now head to the distillery.

With the spread of appellations, the number and power of producers' associations across French vineyards have increased. Although the members of the Bordeaux wine trade have had quality institutions for decades, other areas have moved toward self-governing arrangements and away from the state mechanisms regulating low-end production. The Languedoc, historically known for its bulk wine production, in 1999 ranked fourth in acreage among winegrowing areas in France with AOC, behind Bordeaux, Burgundy, and the Loire Valley. This change led one industry participant to observe that the proliferation of

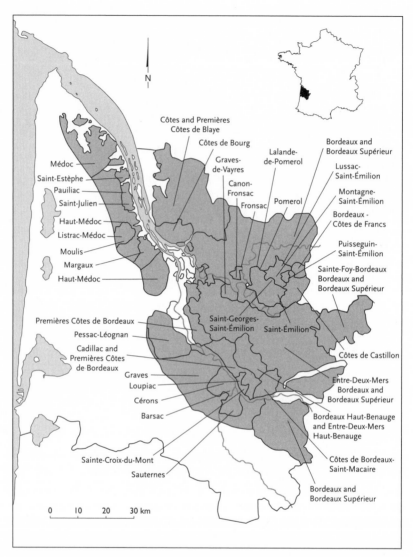

Figure 4. The fifty-seven appellations of Bordeaux.

appellations, *syndicats,* and their officials means now "it is easy to lose count of *Présidents* in the Midi!"[51]

Can consumers really keep track of 470 appellations? "There are so many appellations that I don't even know them all," said Michel Rolland at a panel at the Vinexpo 2004 trade show in Chicago. If this "flying wine-maker," who consults at wineries from Napa to Argentina, finds the French system confusing, then how can the average American consumer cope? It's tough enough remembering the difference between Pouilly-Fuissé and Pouilly-Fumé, recent AOCs such as Orléans and Orléans-Clery.

The popularity of the appellation system among producers has led to its expansion to foodstuffs, which adds to the bureaucratic burden. What used to be a wine club has become a wine, cheese, and lentil club. In July 1990 INAO added appellations for dairy products. France has more than 350 recognized varieties of cheese, and many of them, such as Camembert and Roquefort, use a geographic indication of origin. Although some cheese *syndicats* already existed outside the INAO framework, some producers organized anew to gain the AOC status. The impetus came from a variety of sources: a collective desire to protect their name or product or traditional methods of production, a local crisis, or a desire to increase name recognition.[52] A separate structure was created within the INAO to deal with them. The organization now has separate divisions for wine; cheese and dairy; and other foodstuffs. Another is proposed. By 1999 the list of products with appellations (and associated INAO committees) included poultry from Bresse, lavender from Provence, nuts from Grenoble, green lentils from the Auvergne (Puy), and various olive oils from Provence.

This expansion has left some of the original appellation wine producers feeling upstaged. The self-regulatory framework they devised had worked well for their needs. By 1999, the system had become bogged down with a burgeoning number of applications. Perhaps in consequence, the Ministry of Agriculture, which had previously rubber-stamped the decisions of the INAO, has taken to vetoing requests for new appellations and changes to the regulations, or sending them back for further study. Thus some older members of the wine trade sense a loss of autonomy.[53] But for the producers in the newest appellations, the associations provide greater power, collective control, and recognition than they had under the state-administered system.

-+>-<+-

Anselme Selosse has a plan of his own. Located in the town of Azive in Champagne, Selosse farms thirty-five plots of Chardonnay and makes separate wines from each. In an age of big brands from the region, his is perhaps the ultimate "grower champagne," with limited quantities produced and sold for about $100 a bottle in stores. Selosse heads a group of two hundred independent growers from Alsace to Banyuls to Bordeaux who are dissatisfied with the status quo. But unlike those who have taken to the streets, these appellation members are by and large financially healthy. Their group, Sève (the French word means both "sap" and "vigor"), seeks to return to the roots of the appellation system, in the spirit of its founder, Joseph Capus. Their manifesto calls for an ethical and responsible "refounding" of French viticulture. They dislike commercial yeast strains that they claim make wines taste similar. They dislike the appellation system's process of tasting by committee, arguing that it promotes blandness, uniformity, and mediocrity. They value *terroir* and want to reward winegrowers whose products express it. Their "natural" wines are the latest trend in Parisian wine bars. Whether this approach will contribute to a substantive solution remains to be seen. But the quality and success of their wines will certainly make reformers take these producers seriously.

→>-<-

If the appellation system is broken, why do winemakers keep signing up for it? In political economy, such behavior is known as a collective-action problem: an optimal outcome for an individual or a firm produces a suboptimal outcome for the entire group. Producers in diverse regions have an incentive to apply for an appellation, as the certification usually fetches a premium in the marketplace. But the more producers who sign up, the more unwieldy the apparatus becomes. Moreover, the gradual increase in yields that resulted from the expansion of appellations could be absorbed by the market while demand was also growing. But with the contraction of demand in recent years, the level of overproduction has become unsustainable.

Various members of the wine trade have proposed reforms. René Renou, the former head of the national committee on wines at the INAO, floated the idea of an *appellation d'origine contrôlée d'excellence* (AOCE) in 2004. The two-tier proposal was rejected, however, as it would have devalued the rest of the (nonexcellent) appellations and further complicated an already confusing system. Christian Delpeuch, who held the rotating leadership of the CIVB from 2004 to 2006, declined to serve for a third year, in part out of frustration at his inability to implement reforms in the region. The minister of agriculture at the time, Dominique Bussereau, proposed a National Council of French Winegrowing, which would consolidate all the groups of table-wine producers and those of the appellation winemakers into two federations within the council. If it simply adds another debating chamber with no power and no reform proposals, then this proposal, too, will fall on the scrap heap of reforms.

Some other useful ideas have emerged from the grass roots. The five right-bank appellations of Bordeau that share the word *côtes* in their names[54] merged into one in 2007. The syndicates from Languedoc were trying to form a common front for bargaining with supermarkets over the sale and marketing of both appellation wine and *vin de pays*. They proposed an addition to the labels of both categories of wines: a blue "South of France" logo that would appear on the label of wines from the region, along with the appellation, if any. However, because many of the appellations are not well known, and because appellation producers expect their wines to fetch a higher price than *vin de pays*, an initiative that seems to undercut the importance of the appellation may not be long-lived.

Top-down reform may have the most influence. At the international level, in March 2006, the European Union and the United States resolved a twenty-year dispute about place names and winemaking techniques. The United States will stop using any place names that are protected in France, such as Champagne and Burgundy. However, a grandfather provision allows brands currently using such terms, such as Korbel California Champagne, to continue to do so. France has been able to prevent other EU countries from using such terms. When producers of sparkling wine in northeastern Spain had to stop using the term *champán*, they invented the term *cava* instead. But the United States was not an original signatory to the 1891 Madrid Protocol governing the international registration of trademarks (the protocol took effect in the United States only in 2003), and the EU has finally thrown in the towel on the use of the name. Further, the preliminary accord allowed for American wines made with practices not allowed in the EU, such as using oak chips instead of aging wine in oak barrels, to be sold in Europe after the accord is finalized.

This agreement created the opportunity for a reform of EU winemaking and marketing policy, and Mariann Fischer Boel, the European commissioner for agriculture, seized it. On June 22, 2006, she proposed a "bold reform" to help solve the problems of the low-end wine producers. She proposed to uproot one-eighth of all vineyards in the

EU, thereby decommissioning an area the equivalent of all the vineyards of California; to stop funding "crisis" distillation; and to allow
winemakers more flexibility in making and marketing their wines. For
example, a producer in France that makes a *vin de pays* can currently
market it as Chardonnay only if it is 100 percent Chardonnay from
one region. The new rules may allow *vin de pays* producers to blend
Chardonnay from more than one region and perhaps also to blend in
other grapes. Such blending is standard practice among New World
winemakers. Commissioner Fischer Boel appears to have the resolve;
whether she also has the political muscle to implement her proposals
remains to be seen.

Also in June 2006, the INAO voted to split the wine appellations
into two categories. Regulations for the top appellations will stay the
same, but the second tier will operate under more flexible rules for
winemaking and marketing, such as using oak chips or labeling wines
by grape varieties as well as by appellation. Vitisphere, a French wine
website, called the reform a "revolution."

Reform is in the air, along with a new, more consumer-friendly attitude. Bernard Pomel of the Ministry of Agriculture has observed: "We
have to make wine for consumers, not wine that producers dream
of."[55]

CHAPTER 4

Baptists and Bootleggers

The Strange Bedfellows of American Wine

In December 1995, a fourteen-year-old boy in Kentucky called a store in Los Angeles and ordered some Budweiser, Kendall-Jackson Chardonnay, and Jack Daniel's whiskey to be shipped to his home. Although the purchase of such readily available items for shipment across the country (including the whiskey, which came from neighboring Tennessee) should have at least raised an eyebrow, the clerk processed the order without even asking the age of the person placing it. When the boy opened the shipment in Kentucky, he was surrounded by journalists and camera crews that his father had called in to document the ease of the crime.[1] Within a year, shipping alcohol of any kind to Kentucky had been classified as a felony, on a par with assault, arson, grand theft, and murder. Six other states quickly followed suit. Thus, in 1999, winemakers could ship wine directly to only a dozen states easily and to another dozen with few restrictions. And for shipping to seven states, they risked losing their federal licenses and spending time in jail.

Because of the odd patchwork of state laws, it is easier for a producer to ship a case of wine from Bordeaux to Berlin than from Napa to New Jersey. Consumers, too, have to negotiate local and state laws that can ban the sale of alcohol outright or restrict sale not only by the age of the purchaser but also by time, day of the week, and location. Although some of these barriers are being pruned like a vine after harvest—or, in some cases, uprooted altogether—their roots are deep, and change has been only recent.

PROHIBITION'S VICIOUS HANGOVER

Part of the resistance to wine in America was the bad taste left after the repeal of Prohibition. When Repeal arrived in 1933, vineyard quality had been terribly degraded because of home winemakers' preference for hardy, abundant grapes over good wine grapes. Thus the 1930s saw tremendous surpluses: quality was dismal, and the economy was struggling. In 1934, producers formed the Wine Institute to carry out marketing and consumer education, but with little immediate success: by 1938, the glut was so severe that a federal prorate order was issued, requiring producers to divert almost half of their production to the distillery to make brandy and other fortified sweet wines. California agricultural regulators imposed a levy on producers to market their wines. The excess wine that had been distilled into sweet wines proved more popular than dry wines, further damaging the image of wine as a drink of moderation.

The Central Valley was California's Languedoc. This vast, fertile region produced abundant grapes in the 1930s. But as high yields and quality tend to be inversely correlated, these bountiful harvests often led to severe price competition. Today the area is the world's fourth largest wine region, with 180,000 acres under vine. Even though it comprises only about half of the grape-growing area in California, it accounts for about 80 percent of California's grapes because of high-yielding varieties, new technologies, and hot summers.

In the late 1930s, some growers in the Central Valley took control of the market into their own hands. Grape harvests were abundant, and the prorate and marketing orders had failed, so nineteen large producers, mostly from the Central Valley joined together to create a company that had significant marketing power. Reminiscent of the monopolistic California Wine Association of the turn of the century, the Central California Wineries received financial backing from the Bank of America, which took an equity stake in the company.[2] Through vineyard ownership, contracts with grape growers, and ownership and operation of two winemaking facilities, which included Greystone in St. Helena, the company controlled a large share of California wine production—too large, in the view of the federal authorities. The Justice Department indicted the bankers and the wine producers for a "conspiracy to raise, fix, control, and stabilize" prices. Although the charges were dropped, the company ceased to exist and sold its assets to a competitor in 1942.

The Second World War stabilized the domestic wine market through the price controls of the Office of Price Administration and the

FROM BULK TO BOTTLE: *MIS EN BOUTEILLE AU CHÂTEAU . . . À L'AMERICAINE*

One of the unintended consequences of the wartime Office of Price Administration controls was a shift to bottled wine away from bulk, which actually improved wine quality. At the time, the industry relied on sales of bulk wine, which was shipped by rail and tanker trucks to 1,500 bottling facilities across the country. The price ceilings, which applied to wine but not to grapes, slashed the already thin margins on bulk wine. The price ceilings on bottled wine offered the wineries a margin two to five times that of the bulk-wine price. "The result was that, with the onset of the war and OPA regulations, the bulk wine market all but disappeared," says Louis Gomberg ("Analytical Perspectives on the California Wine Industry," *California Winemen Oral History Project*, 1990, 14–15). While this development may have been only a wartime phenomenon, it showed the producers the added value of bottling at the source. Moreover, they had an incentive to improve quality because their names were now appearing on the finished product.

diversion of grapes to food production to help the war effort. As soon as the war ended, surpluses returned, and between 1949 and 1952 the state imposed more controls on the sale of bulk wine. In 1961, this time under federal law, a new program diverted 40 million gallons of surplus into distillation and industrial uses.[3] The plan lasted only two years after growers objected, and collective efforts to mop up the surplus over the next decade met with failure.

The winemaker during this period was seen as a "magic chef" who could transform bad grapes into good wine. Many growers in the 1950s and 1960s grew the bland Thompson Seedless variety because they had three outlets for them: in July they could sell them as table grapes; in August they could dry them and sell them as raisins; or they could leave them on the vines until September and sell them to the wineries. The wine historian Leon Adams summed up the situation: "Growers in the [San Joaquin] valley saw no reason to plant wine-grape varieties, which have only one use—to make wine."[4]

William Bonetti drove to Modesto, the site of the Gallo winemaking facility, to interview for a job as winemaker in 1949. He recalled that, as he was being shown the facility, he was told, "Experiment in the lab. Do anything you want. If you have an idea, try it in the lab, prove it. And if it's worthwhile, then we will proceed with it." He signed on immediately. "That's exciting, you know, for a young man. . . . I started working as a technologist."[5] Science and technology were considered unquestionably beneficial, and applying advanced chemistry to wine-making led to a wider array of products. Bonetti would experiment all day and then present several choices to Julio Gallo at the end of the day to sample. But the real pull came from the sales team, led by Julio's brother Ernest, who presented the winemakers with its assessment of consumer demands. In response, the lab technicians concocted a wide variety of wine-based beverages, some of which succeeded while others flopped. A notable failure was a whiskey sour that contained no whiskey, marketed under the label Sporting Wine. Much more popular was a flavor-enhanced, high-alcohol mix marketed as Thunderbird. This drink, with a base of white port of 21 percent alcohol and a lemon flavor, had unprecedented success, thanks in part to aggressive market-ing and a low price, but consumers saw it as a "skid row" wine.[6] This wine was not a drink of moderation according to the Jeffersonian ideal: it was a product that gave a cheap buzz. Thunderbird sales were strong, and by 1967 Gallo had become the biggest wine producer in the United States. But the demand for sweet wines from Gallo and others soon declined, and in 1968, dry "table" wines outsold sweet dessert wines for the first time.[7] A transition to quality was under way.

-+->-<+-

When Robert Mondavi opened his winery in Napa Valley in 1966, it was the first new Napa winery in thirty years. His family had been in the wine business for generations, at the Charles Krug winery. But Mondavi clashed with other family members: he wanted to expand the company, while his younger brother, Peter, was more conservative. After a heated exchange at a family gathering in 1965, Robert punched Peter. Robert then took a paid leave from the company and went on his first trip to Europe, where he visited several winemaking regions with long pedigrees. When he returned to Napa Valley to open his own win-ery, his approach placed an emphasis on quality that had been lacking in much of California, even in Napa.

Even so, Mondavi did not have the market for quality wine all to himself. The year 1972 saw an investment boom in California's vine-yards. The Bank of America produced an influential analysis of the wine market that predicted rapid growth in both production and con-sumption.[8] The report pointed to the sharp rise in production in the preceding few years, from 203 million gallons (7.6 million hL) in 1967 to 337 million gallons (12.7 million hL) in 1972, a gain of 10.7 percent per year. The report forecast that this trend would continue or even accelerate, predicting that annual domestic per capita wine consumption would rise from 1.5 gallons in 1970 to around 10 gallons in 1980. Even though this projection proved wildly off the mark (per capita wine consumption in the United States in 2001 was only 2.3 gallons), the report sparked a period of easy money and new entrants to the industry. Rodney Strong, who owned a winery in Sonoma at the time, commented that the report "just set off the conservative financial community into a rampage." Investing in wineries "was the rage in the mid and late 60s and into the 70s. It was the golden age of growth. . . . we were growing forty or fifty percent a year because we were on such a small base."[9] Many of the small investors in the wine industry were successful doctors, dentists, lawyers, investment bankers, and even dance choreographers (such as Strong) or film directors seeking a change. The number of wineries in California rose from 240 in 1970 to 550 in 1983.[10]

Drawn by the prospect of big gains, large companies from outside the industry started to invest in California wine. In 1969 Heublein, a conglomerate based in Connecticut that owned Smirnoff Vodka as well as Kentucky Fried Chicken, bought United Vintners and Beaulieu Vineyards to become the second largest producer. In 1971, Seagram bought the portion of the Paul Masson winery that it did not already own. In 1977, the Coca-Cola Company took aim at Gallo by buying the quality Napa producer Sterling and the mid-sized Monterey Vineyard and building a massive new Taylor California facility (seeking to add to its Taylor Wine holding of New York). Other firms, such as Pillsbury and Nestlé, were also attracted to the industry. All of these large firms brought with them a corporate culture focused on brands, competitive marketing campaigns and strategies, and a desire for quick and stable returns. The idea of wine as a brand product was growing. But that wine would be part and parcel of a conglomerate. Where was the corporate synergy between Pillsbury biscuits, chicken drumsticks, and premium wine?

→>–<–

The rising quality of American wines received prominent international recognition at a now-famous tasting in Paris in 1976. An English wine merchant based in Paris, Steven Spurrier, organized a tasting of American wines to reaffirm ties between France and America on the two-hundredth anniversary of U.S. independence. He assembled a high-profile list of French tasters, including the inspector general of the INAO, the secretary

general of the Syndicat des Grands Crus Classés, several critics, the owners of two Michelin three-star restaurants, and the sommelier from a
third in the elegant rooms of the Hotel Intercontinental. George Taber of
Time magazine, the only journalist who accepted Spurrier's invitation to
the event, recounts that Spurrier announced to the judges after they had
arrived that he had decided to include some French wines alongside the
American upstarts.[11] Spurrier also announced that the labels would be
hidden to make for a blind tasting, and "no one demurred," according to
Taber.

The judges started swirling and sniffing the reds and the whites. "Ah,
back to France," one taster remarked. Another exclaimed, "The magnifi-
cence of France. It soars! Certainly a premier grand cru of Bordeaux."
They assigned their ratings accordingly. Taber, who had a sheet that dis-
closed the wine names, recalls that he could see a story breaking.[12] When
the labels were revealed, a California Chardonnay (Chateau Montelena)
and Cabernet Sauvignon (Stag's Leap) had taken the top spots. In fact, six
out of the eleven top wines in the tasting were American.[13] The praise
lavished on the best wines that the tasters had assumed to be French
turned into compliments for the American winemakers, while some of
the derision for poor wines turned out to be directed at white Burgundies.
The tasters were shocked, and some even disputed the results. However,
another blind tasting later that year confirmed the results.[14] "Not bad for
kids from the sticks," commented Jim Barrett, Montelena's general manager.[15] California quality wines had earned their place among the world's
top wines. The struggle with the soil had finally been won.[16]

With this newfound recognition of quality, California producers had
to decide how to market and label their wines. Would they identify them
by growing region, as was European practice, or by grape variety? Or
would they create brand names that glossed over viticultural issues altogether?

Because decades of belief in the "magic chef" winemaker had consolidated much power in the lab, wine-grape growers had to fight for
recognition of the vineyard's role in making quality wine. Over the
1970s, growers succeeded in negotiating higher prices for their grapes,
overcoming the dominance of the winery buyers, and obtained the formal recognition of growing areas.

Gallo and other large firms dominated the pricing of wine grapes in
the early 1970s. The State Marketing News Service produced a "crush
report" listing grape prices in the state that served as benchmarks in
negotiations between growers and wineries. Unknown to the growers,

however, big wineries could manipulate the benchmark price simply by making an offer to purchase the grapes. As a result, the price offered was often below the growers' cost. Andy Beckstoffer, a prominent grower in Napa Valley, recalled that buyers also dragged their feet over making payments: "With Allied Grape Growers, for example, you would deliver grapes in October, you would get your first check in March, and you would finally get paid in full in the following October, so that it was not only the price, it was also the payment terms that really caused us a lot of problems. That was 1975."[17] In response, growers in premium regions started to organize. The state started producing price data that were less easily manipulated, and pricing shifted toward a "bottle-price formula," whereby the growers were paid for their grapes on the basis of the final price of the wine in the bottle.[18]

The most significant factor in achieving greater recognition for growers was academic research. Researchers at the University of California—Davis started to develop an American notion of *terroir* in the 1940s. In the Department of Viticulture and Enology, researchers conducted extensive studies of the various growing regions of California. Over five years, Albert Winkler and his student Maynard Amerine made controlled, small batches of wine with grapes from around the state. They found consistent variations among the growing areas and hypothesized that these variations came from differences in climate, particularly temperature. They divided the state into five growing zones based on a heat-index formula: every degree over 50 degrees Fahrenheit per day counted as a "degree day." Zone I had an average of 2,500 degree days; for zone 5, the number was 4,000. Not only did the grapes in the cooler regions ripen more slowly, but chemical and sensory tests of the batches displayed variations as well. These zones, and the number of degree days in a growing area, still serve as common standards in California grape production.[19]

Despite this early academic research on the importance of growing areas, it was only in the 1970s that formal recognition of the vineyards arrived, through the joint efforts of winemakers and growers in the premium areas. In 1975, there were only loose regulations on using place names, such as Napa Valley, and grape varieties on the label. For example, at that time, if a wine was labeled as Cabernet Sauvignon on the label, the bottle had to contain only 51 percent Cabernet Sauvignon. The idea of delimiting growing areas in the name of quality ironically came from E. & J. Gallo Company, better known for its Thunderbird and jug wines. Gallo proposed a North Coast growing area that would encompass fourteen counties and extend as far north as Mendocino

County. Under this proposal, wine made from grapes grown in this area could note the fact on the label, although under the Gallo proposal not all the grapes would have to come from the area. The Wine Institute, the largest trade group, backed the proposal, which was sent to the Bureau of Alcohol, Tobacco, and Firearms for approval.

Such a broadly defined growing zone was controversial because it ran counter to the research from UC Davis and the practice in the French vineyards suggesting that the characteristics of the immediate growing area, the *terroir*, were most important in determining the character of the wine. Andy Beckstoffer was one grower who opposed the Gallo proposal. As head of the newly organized Napa Valley Grape Growers Association, he sought a narrower demarcation of growing areas, particularly in Napa Valley.

With Gallo, the largest producing firm, and the Wine Institute, the statewide industry organization, in favor of the broader designation, Beckstoffer had to seek other allies for his cause. A good candidate was the Napa Valley Vintners Association, a group of quality producers. But Beckstoffer recalls that the Vintners Association rejected the growers' overtures, taking the attitude that growers should not concern themselves with the issue.[20] With the growers thus relegated to second-class status as farmers, Beckstoffer decided to ally with agricultural institutions to advance the group's cause to the highest levels of policymaking. Thus the Growers Association turned to the Napa County Farm Bureau and easily pushed through a policy position in favor of a stronger and narrower delimitation of growing areas. The head of the Napa Farm Bureau, who was also the head of the Grape Policy Committee of the California Farm Bureau, was sympathetic to the Napa growers' position and brought about its adoption by the statewide association.

Because California produced nine out of ten bottles of American wine, the American Farm Bureau generally deferred to the state-level organization on grape-growing matters. In 1975, Beckstoffer flew to Chicago to meet the president of the American Farm Bureau to solidify the growers' position. With this endorsement, Beckstoffer and the executive director of the Farm Bureau went to Washington to meet with the head of wine policy at the Bureau of Alcohol, Tobacco, and Firearms to discuss the growing zones.

In 1976 the BATF held four hearings with industry and consumer representatives, with the goal of setting standards for clearer labeling of wine. The discussions of the proposed definitions and boundaries of the growing areas were contentious. The BATF called a wide range of witnesses, including producers, growers, trade-association directors, and even some critics and journalists. Following the hearings, the BATF issued new rules on the use of grape varieties on labels and established procedures for defining an American Viticultural Area, or AVA.[21] Whereas previous geographic indications had conformed to state or county boundaries, the new viticultural areas could span counties or nestle completely inside them. For a wine to state the AVA on the label, at least 85 percent of the grapes used had to come from the area. Tightening these definitions gave increased power and status to the growers. Beckstoffer commented triumphantly of the grape growers: "We're now part of the deal; we're now part of the wine industry."[22]

Although the new AVA designations did grant growers and growing areas greater recognition, they were toothless compared to the rules for French appellations and quickly became weakened. The BATF established procedures by which any interested party—not just growers or vintners—could petition to establish an AVA. The petitioner had to present evidence that the name was locally or nationally known as a viticultural area; historical or contemporary evidence that the boundaries were as specified; and evidence relating to geological or microclimate features (such as soil, elevation, climate, and physical features) that distinguished the proposed area from surrounding areas. Thus AVAs could be either small and reflective of variations in growing climates, or vague and meaningless marketing devices. This new legal framework ended up accommodating Beckstoffer and the Napa producers as well as Gallo, with its request for a vast North Coast AVA. Unlike the French appellations, AVA regulations placed no controls on grape varieties planted, yields, use of irrigation, or any winemaking practices, and did not require tastings. The BATF was no INAO.

The Napa Valley growers and producers struggled over setting the boundaries of the new AVA. The Napa River flows between two mountain ranges for thirty miles through a broad valley and ultimately drains into the San Francisco Bay. The natural borders for the viticultural area would have been the edges of the valley floor, but vineyards had also been planted on many hillsides, such as Howell Mountain and Mount Veeder. After a debate, the growers voted 97 to 8 to limit the Napa Valley AVA to the watershed of the Napa River, which included the hillsides, and the vintners agreed. Yet, Beckstoffer recalls, the final proposal presented to the BATF extended the AVA beyond the Napa watershed area and over the ridge to the east to include the Pope Valley and Wooden Valley. These regions had little geographic or viticultural connection with the Napa

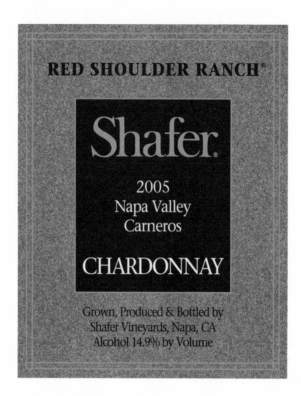

Valley, although grapes from the Pope Valley had traditionally been blended with those from Napa. Beckstoffer, who did not attend the final meeting, suggests that Mondavi and other vintners were responsible for pushing the AVA boundary eastward to include almost the whole county. "But the whole appellation system is so political. I mean, it's just so unbelievably political. It's supposed to be based on geographic features and viticultural characteristics and it's not—it's political. So what happens in the Napa Valley is they set it as the whole of Napa County including Chiles Valley and Pope Valley, and that's ridiculous," Beckstoffer lamented.[23] On February 27, 1981, Napa Valley became the second AVA (petitioners for Augusta in Missouri beat them to the first spot).

By the end of 1983, forty-one AVAs had been approved. The Gallo proposal for the sprawling North Coast AVA was one of them, receiving approval in 1983, and in 1990 it was modified to include several more counties. The total North Coast area now exceeds 3 million acres. More than 160 AVAs are on the books: the recent trend has been

THE POLITICS OF AN AMERICAN LABEL

1 Vintage: In the past, for any wine to qualify as a vintage wine, 95 percent of the grapes had to come from the harvest of the vintage year. A recent reform has lowered this requirement to 85 percent for wines not from specific growing areas.

2 Name: The name of the brand or the producer.

3 Variety: At least 75 percent of the wine must be made from the grape variety specified on the label.

4 American Viticultural Area: At least 85 percent of the grapes used must be from the stated AVA, in this case Carneros. Wines from Napa are also identified as coming from the Napa Valley.

5 Single vineyard: If a single vineyard is specified, 95 percent of the grapes must come from that vineyard. This wine comes from the Red Shoulder Ranch vineyard.

6 Alcohol by volume: Above 14 percent, the stated percentage of alcohol must be accurate to plus or minus 1 percent; below 14 percent, it must be accurate to within plus or minus 1.5 percent.

7 Net contents: For bottles under one liter in size, the contents must be stated in milliliters, and the measurement must be exact.

8 Government warning (on rear label): Mandatory health warning.

9 Sulfite warning: Mandatory if sulfites are added (see chapter 6).

toward creating large regions that have more future potential than past performance. On January 6, 2006, the thumping 2.3 million-acre Texoma AVA in Texas, north of Dallas, gained approval. At the time of approval it had only 55 acres planted, and four wineries. And Washington State has been bulking up, with the 68,500-acre Rattlesnake Hills area gaining approval as the state's ninth AVA in March 2006.[24]

Given this dilution of the significance of the AVA, several growers and winemakers have sought recognition of the smaller growing areas in Napa. Now fourteen AVAs nestle inside the Napa Valley AVA, named for distinctive growing areas, such as Rutherford and Oakville. And many producers have turned to vineyard designation for even greater awareness of the *terroir*. Growers certainly pushed for the increased recognition of their plots. Beckstoffer argues: "The thing that's not political is vineyard designation. It is a specific piece of ground, so you know exactly what's going to happen in that piece of ground. . . . So the new ultimate assurance of quality and consistency to the consumer is vineyard designation." Bottles from any AVA in Napa (such as Rutherford) are also labeled as Napa Valley wines, which furthers recognition of the smaller areas' names. In Sonoma, bottles from the smaller AVAs (such as the Russian River Valley) do not have to bear the Sonoma label, and thus these names are less widely recognized.

The new federal regulations sought to provide more precise information to the consumer about the contents of the bottle. If the grape variety is specified on the label, 75 percent of the grapes used must be of that variety; if the AVA is specified, 85 percent of the fruit must come from that AVA; and if a single vineyard is mentioned, 95 percent of the fruit must come from that vineyard.

The percentages stipulated above allow the producers considerable leeway in labeling, sometimes to the disadvantage of the consumer. Grape variety, for which the widest deviation is permitted, is arguably the least important: although diluting wine from one grape variety with 25 percent of something else can dramatically alter its character, many of the finest wines are blends of several grapes. But when AVA and vineyard-level designations allow the addition of any quantity of fruit from outside the area, the resulting wine cannot truly be said to be characteristic of that area. Producers counter this argument by pointing out that those in competitive AVAs have little incentive to dilute their wines with inferior ones from outside the AVA.

Another somewhat questionable stipulation on the label is the vintage. In California, Hollywood stars are not the only ones who can fudge their age: only 95 percent of the grapes for AVA vintage wines are required to come from the vintage on the label. Vintage is controversial in California, with some producers and even some wine critics arguing that the consistency of production from year to year makes it unimportant. In 2006 the Wine Institute successfully lobbied federal regulators to reduce the requirement to 85 percent vintage grapes for non-AVA wines.

-+>-<+-

With the soil having shown its potential, the California wine industry experienced a surprising stagnation in the 1980s. Yet while the increase in consumption slowed, the wines consumed changed significantly. For high-volume producers, it was a time once again for innovation in the lab as opposed to the vineyard, as producers introduced several new wine products, such as wine coolers. For the quality producers, it was a time for improving technique and refining the focus on quality. Particularly important was a new emphasis on quality grape varieties.

Even though grape varieties had appeared on wine labels since Frank Schoonmaker, an early and influential wine writer and merchant, put them there in the 1940s, American consumers and winemakers could not decide whether to refer to wine by the name of the grapes or the name of the ground where they grew. In some cases, producers still used the place names of Europe, such as "Chablis" or "hearty Burgundy," even though the grapes came from California. Stating the grape variety seemed more truthful (though not necessarily absolutely so). But because the familiar French wines did not state grape varieties on the label, consumers' knowledge of grapes, even "noble" varieties such as Cabernet Sauvignon and Chardonnay, was weak. Even in the mid-1980s, the industry publication *Impact* did not differentiate wines beyond the categories of red, white, and rosé.[25]

To distinguish their wines, several producers started making aggressive varietal claims, leading the wines to be called "fighting varietals."[26] These wines generally sold for $4 to $7, were sealed with a corks rather than screw tops to signal better quality, and had a taste akin to that of the grapes they came from. Jess Jackson, the founder of Kendall-Jackson Vineyard Estates and one of the leaders of the fighting varietals, claimed to want to use only "the best of the best" in his Chardonnay. Undermining the recognition of the growing area, he took the grapes from several growing areas. Cabernet Sauvignon and Chardonnay emerged as the most recognizable red and white varieties, though white wines outsold the reds during the 1980s. The fighting varietals raised the price consumers were willing to pay and raised their expectations. The strategy, however, ultimately proved somewhat self-defeating. In the longer run, Chardonnay and other labeled varieties came to be seen as undifferentiated commodities, competing on the basis of price rather than quality.

-+>-<+-

Low-end producers continued to rely on innovation and product diversification to avoid direct price competition. One successful introduction—in a "fortuitous accident"—was White Zinfandel.[27] Zinfandel, a red grape widely planted in the 1980s and 1990s, is often considered a variety indigenous to the United States. Charles Sullivan, among others, has contested this claim and followed Zinfandel's origins back to Long Island in the nineteenth century and thence to Italy, where genetic testing has revealed the grape to be related to the Primitivo of Italy.[28] Subsequently, the researcher Carole Meredith has traced it back farther to the Crljenak, a grape variety indigenous to Croatia's Dalmatian Coast.

Regardless of its origin, under the California sun, the Zinfandel grape makes a strong red wine, high in alcohol. In the 1970s, some

BATF TO TTB: COLLECTING AND PROTECTING

Unlike the quality appellation producers of France, who, through the INAO, have access to the minister of agriculture, American wine producers are governed by the unsympathetic Department of the Treasury. Until a bureaucratic reorganization in 2002, the regulatory authority for wine was the Treasury's Bureau of Alcohol, Tobacco, and Firearms (BATF), which was known primarily as an enforcement agency. When law enforcement and counterterrorism responsibilities were transferred to the Department of Justice in 2002, the duties of collecting revenue and protecting the consumer were assigned to the new Alcohol and Tobacco Tax and Trade Bureau, or TTB.

The TTB collects excise taxes on wine, beer, and spirits as well as on tobacco. These taxes accounted for $16 billion in federal government revenue in 2005 (on total sales of $2.1 trillion), with wine accounting for over $2 billion. The Treasury also issues federal licenses to each owner, who must post bond money to ensure assets for tax payments. The officials at TTB also regulate the use of specific terms on the label, such as the vintage or place name; establish and enforce hygienic standards for wine; and approve the designations of American Viticultural Areas. They also represent American winemaking in many international organizations, although no longer in the Paris-based Office International de la Vigne et du Vin, as the U.S. withdrew from the organization in 2000.

The current regulatory style is akin to a night watchman's. Producers must keep thorough records, and inspectors are entitled to make on-site inspections once a month, although they rarely do so. TTB officials say that the competitive nature of the California wine industry encourages thorough record keeping. In the event of an infraction, they often receive a tip-off from a competitor: Rabbit Ridge of Healdsburg, California, paid $810,000 in fines for two violations relating to mislabeling wine and inaccurate record keeping in 2001.

---

producers were trying to maximize the strength of their red Zinfandels. Bob Trinchero, of the Sutter Home Winery, was among them.[29] To strengthen the red wine, Trinchero removed the light juice from the first press. Instead of discarding the 550 gallons of juice, he decided to make a "blush" wine, or a white wine made from red grapes. A friend suggested naming the product *oeil de perdrix*, or "eye of the partridge," a colloquial name for rosé wines in French. Trinchero put *Oeil de Perdrix* on the label and sold the thin, dry blush wine out of his winery.

To placate the BATF, which prohibited the use of foreign terms on labels without a translation, Trinchero added "A White Zinfandel Wine." Sales were slow. In the third year of production, the fermentation process accidentally "stuck" (the yeasts gave out before the sugars), and the resulting wine was left with high sugar levels along with the pink hue. That year, the White Zinfandel was the first Sutter Home wine to sell out, and the same happened in the following year. According to Roger Trinchero, Bob's younger brother, "We were sitting around, sort of scratching our heads, wondering what was going on. We weren't the brightest guys in the world, but eventually it dawned on us that maybe we should make more white zinfandel."[30] They started purchasing fruit and increased production to 20,000 cases. By 1983, Sutter Home alone was producing 3 million cases of White Zinfandel.

Among other bulk producers, experimentation continued. In 1984, Seagram's introduced a wine cooler (a sweet, sparkling, wine-based beverage) to compete with similar products from Gallo, Canandaigua, and Brown-Forman. The American palate had taken a turn for the sweet once again.

-*><-*-

Even though wine was reaching new markets, the struggle with social attitudes was not over. In 1980, Cari Lightner, age thirteen, was killed by a driver under the influence of alcohol. Her mother, Candy Lightner, a thirty-three-year-old real estate broker and mother of two other children, founded the activist organization Mothers Against Drunk Driving (MADD). Because as many as half of annual road deaths at the time were alcohol related, the movement instantly found a wide following. By 1985, MADD had 320 chapters, 600,000 volunteers and donors, and a budget of $10 million. Candy Lightner was named one of "seven who succeeded" by *Time* Magazine in its 1985 "Man of the Year" feature and one of five "original thinkers" of the 1980s by *Life* magazine in 1989. MADD also inspired the formation of a sister organization of students, SADD. Lightner became the figurehead for the anti–drunk driving movement.[31]

The success of grass-roots movements such as MADD led to nationwide policy responses. Under the Reagan administration, in a classic example of top-down policymaking, the 1984 federal budget made the release of national highway funds to the states conditional on the states' establishing a minimum drinking age of twenty-one. Federal highway funds represent a large source of revenue for states, and they all complied, reluctantly or otherwise.[32]

Political pressure led to further tightening of the laws restricting drinking and driving. Many states lowered the permissible blood alcohol levels for driving and imposed stricter penalties, including fines and the suspension of driver's licenses, for those caught in violation. The FDA took further action by requiring government warnings about the

TABLE 4. FEDERAL EXCISE TAX ON WINE,
PER GALLON

	November 1, 1951– December 31, 1990 ($)	January 1, 1991– Present ($)
Under 14% alcohol	0.17	1.07
14.1–21% alcohol	0.67	1.57
Sparkling wine[a]	3.40	3.40

[a]Since January 1, 1955.
SOURCE: Alcohol and Tobacco Tax and Trade Bureau.

dangers of consuming alcohol in excess, while operating machinery, or while pregnant. At the same time, drug laws were tightened, as were restrictions on the sale of tobacco to minors. Thus wine, like all alcoholic beverages, became associated in the public mind with crime, drug abuse, and other products deemed dangerous and in need of regulation, such as tobacco and guns.

Congress did not want to appear passive in this campaign and decided to raise the excise tax on alcohol. The tax on wine, which varies by alcohol content, had until then been relatively low. In 1991, however, the tax on wine (below 14 percent alcohol) went from $0.17 per gallon to $1.07 per gallon, a 529 percent increase (see table 4).[33]

A provision was included in the legislation, however, that granted an exemption to small "mom and pop" wineries. Senator Mark Hatfield (R-Oregon) sponsored an amendment that allowed small producers—those with annual production of less than 150,000 gallons (or 62,500 cases of 750 mL bottles)—to pay the old rate for the first 100,000 gallons of production (about 42,000 cases).[34] This provision saved small wineries $90,000 on the first 100,000 gallons produced—about the equivalent of a good winemaker's annual salary, or the interest on more than $1 million in loans.

As a result of these social movements and the shift in cultural and legal conceptions of wine, consumption stagnated, competition focused on price, and margins shrank. The investments in wine by diversified firms failed to pan out, and, as the alcohol business became stigmatized, most of them abandoned ship. Heublein sold its assets to Allied Grape Growers, Coca-Cola sold its holdings to Seagram, and Pillsbury and RJR Nabisco also beat a hasty retreat. But just when wine appeared to have been vanquished by a latter-day temperance movement, television saved it.

+>-<+

In November 1991 the popular current-affairs program *60 Minutes* aired a twelve-minute story on health that focused on the "French paradox." Residents of Mediterranean France were found to have lower rates of heart disease than Americans in spite of eating more dietary fat. The difference was tentatively attributed to the French habit of drinking a moderate amount of wine—and red wine in particular. This finding completely reframed the debate on wine, as wine proponents could now point to indications of some actual health benefits. The producers sought to popularize the notion that wine, consumed in moderation and with meals, as in the European tradition, is a healthy addition to the daily diet.[35]

Media coverage of this finding spurred a strong growth in demand. A number of medical studies—some funded by the industry—investigated the health benefits of red wine. Some drinkers were attracted to wine for the first time—including Robert Parker's mother. Parker, the foremost American wine critic, who reviews thousands of wines every year, grew up in the dairy-farming country of Maryland in a household that did not drink wine. After watching the *60 Minutes* episode, he reported, his mom gave him a call and said, "Bob, I hear red wine is good for me. Can you recommend one?"[36] As consumers across America started reaching for red wine, growers responded accordingly: red grape plantings soon outstripped those of white grapes.

During the 1990s, the small wineries that focused on quality production increased in number, and their products commanded higher prices. One was Colgin Cellars. Ann Colgin, an art and antiques dealer from Florida, purchased ten acres in Napa Valley in 1992 and hired a celebrity winemaker to oversee production. The emphasis on quality, the limited production (only two hundred cases), and favorable ratings from the critics pushed the price of her Cabernet Sauvignon to $300 a bottle. Sold only through a mailing list, the wine soon appeared at auction for $500 per bottle (at the charity Auction Napa Valley, it set a record when one lot of six three-liter bottles sold for $850,000). Buyers with wealth derived from the equity price boom of the late 1990s drove winery and acreage prices sharply upward, attracted more investment, and led to more wineries making stratospherically priced specialty wines.

Smaller winemakers emphasized quality and also rejected the 1960s faith in technology and science. Although they viewed the arrival of stainless steel tanks and small French oak barrels for fermentation as a distinct improvement over the concrete and redwood vats common after World War II, they often advocated minimal tampering with the innate flavors of the wine. Miljenko (Mike) Grgich, who made the

Chateau Montelena Chardonnay that won the 1976 Paris tasting, does not use filtration at his own winery, Grgich Hills. "Our philosophy is to keep in the wine whatever comes from the grapes, like everything is in whole wheat bread," he said in 1993. "Our wines do have body, and because of the body they have longevity."[37] This view prevailed in the quality wine-producing areas. Other high-end producers started to use organic and even biodynamic farming techniques (see chapter 6).

Some of the big winemakers began using the profits from their bulk brands to finance small-scale quality production. "Underneath Chateau Souverain we have Beringer White Zinfandel supporting the winery. Underneath the Meridian winery we have the Napa Ridge wines supporting the winery," recounted Mike Moone, former CEO of Beringer.[38]

The increased emphasis on quality meant an increased focus on single-vineyard bottling. Since the 1966 vintage, Heitz Wine Cellars had made a "Martha's Vineyard" cuvée, named for a vineyard owned by Tom and Martha May in Oakville, which became one of Heitz's most sought-after wines. Other winemakers followed suit, notably Paul Draper at Ridge, identifying specific vineyards on the label even when they were owned by independent growers. The trend picked up steam in the 1990s, particularly with Zinfandels, as producers such as Rosenblum put single vineyards on the label—twenty of them in the 2004 vintage. "We're finding that the vineyards have characteristics of their own that we really enjoy," Jeff Cohn, the enologist at Rosenblum, said in 1998.[39] Is it too confusing for the consumer? "We wouldn't do it if people didn't want it," Kent Rosenblum told me. "It's a challenge to carry them all," his New York distributor told me, also noting that restaurants may shy away from single-vineyard offerings because of the limited supply: "If the customer wants to offer the same wine on their list [repeatedly], it's not for them."[40]

Whether single-vineyard labeling is overkill is a matter of opinion. Certainly Burgundy values location highly, as evidenced by the large numbers of tiny vineyards, and many supporters of *terroir* feel California's vineyards have comparable diversity. Single-vineyard bottlings have proliferated for Pinot Noir, perhaps even more so than for Zinfandel. But the trend in California has been met with skepticism. Gary Farrel of Rochioli has been quoted as saying that it is "more marketing driven than winemaker driven." And Steve Heimoff jokes that every extra word a vintner can squeeze onto a front label is worth an additional $5.[41]

The competitive high-end wine market remains highly fragmented (see table 5). The trend toward small is not reflected in the distributor structure. The top twenty wineries control 80 percent of production;

TABLE 5. U.S. WINE CATEGORIES AND
BESTSELLERS IN EACH, 2004

Regular Premium ($3–7 Bottle at Retail)			Super Premium/Deluxe (> $7)		
	Average Retail Price ($)	Market Share (%)		Average Retail Price ($)	Market Share (%)
Beringer	6.90	2.9	Kendall-Jackson	13.65	1.4
Kendall-Jackson	13.65	1.4	Moët & Chandon	43.95	0.2
			Clos du Bois	12.65	0.6
Yellow Tail	6.85	2.4	Rosemount	10.00	0.7
Woodbridge	6.75	2.4	Beaulieu Vineyards	10.75	0.6
Franzia	1.65	8.5	Top 5	14.15	3.5
Top 5	4.80	17.6			

SOURCE: *The U.S. Wine Market: Impact Databank, Review, and Forecast* (New York: M. Shanken Communications, 2005).

the top fifty control almost 95 percent.[42] Only thirty wineries made more than 250,000 cases in 2005.

NAME POLITICS

One problem for producers in promoting an awareness of growing areas has been that some brand names have conflicted with the names of smaller AVAs. An early case in Napa Valley was over the name Stags Leap. With a name derived from Native American tradition, this craggy rock outcropping provided the backdrop for a distinctive and superlative growing area for Cabernet Sauvignon—indeed, it was the Cabernet from Stag's Leap Wine Cellars that triumphed in Paris in 1976. Confusion understandably arose with the opening of Stags' Leap Winery— note the placement of the apostrophes—and when petitioners sought AVA status for the region in the mid 1980s, they scrapped the apostrophe altogether, opting for Stags Leap.[43] Stags' Leap Winery now belongs to Beringer Blass Wine Estates, whose promotional materials claim that the winery dates from 1893.

But the Stag's Leap case was a dispute between two producers who already existed. In the wake of this dispute, the BATF ruled that producers who had a geographic name in their brand prior to the formation of a similarly named AVA could continue to use the name. That decision seemed to appease producers, but it created a loophole that in one case was dramatically exploited.

Fred T. Franzia and his Bronco Wine Company, one of the largest producers in the United States, bought Rutherford Vineyards, in the Rutherford AVA in Napa Valley, in 1996. The production of the winery was small: three thousand cases a year. Because Franzia's business model is based on volume—indeed, the company later created "Two Buck Chuck," one of the biggest-volume wine brands—this purchase was unusual (although he did own Napa Creek and Domaine Napa and in 2000 purchased the Napa Ridge brand from Beringer). However, the purpose behind his new acquisition soon became clear: Franzia planned to change the geographic indication on the label to "California" instead of Rutherford and raise production to as much as 18 million cases by trucking in fruit from the low-cost area of Lodi, south of Sacramento, and bottling it at a huge new bottling facility in Napa.[44] The total production in Napa Valley was only around 10 million cases at that time. Franzia had pleaded no contest in 1993 to a federal indictment that he passed off cheap Zinfandel from the Central Valley as wine from premium fruit. He and Bronco paid $3 million in fines, and he had to withdraw from the wine industry for five years. With the Rutherford Vineyards ploy, Franzia was planning to state on the label that the grapes had come from Lodi, but the information was to be set in small type, while the brand name, Rutherford Vineyards, would be set in large type. Such an action would represent a serious devaluation of the Rutherford name (and, by implication, Napa's too). Franzia's frequent retort was, "You don't expect your Hawaiian Punch from Hawaii or your London Fog from London."

The crux of the matter was Federal Regulation 439i, which dated from July 7, 1986. Before that date, wines could contain less than 75 percent grapes from the growing area even if their name was the same as that of the AVA, a situation that was not allowed after the regulation. "This was the worst decision the ATF ever made," said Tom Shelton, past president of the Napa Valley Vintners Association and CEO of Joseph Phelps. "This created a secondary market for these labels."[45] Dennis Groth, another Napa producer, told the *Wall Street Journal* that Franzia had described himself as "a buzzard, swooping over the Napa Valley looking for some little carcass to pick up."[46]

Bronco brazenly extolled the virtues of *terroir* and ran an advertising campaign under the slogan "It's the vineyard," with a photo of rolling hills, crisscrossing rows of vines, trees, and a small pond. The photo, however, did not come from Rutherford Vineyards; it was instead an unauthorized picture taken from the veranda of Joseph

Phelps, a producer of acclaimed wines in the area. Phelps threatened to sue Franzia for trademark infringement, and Franzia eventually withdrew the ad.

Despite his commercial success, with 2005 revenues of more than $300 million, Franzia was not popular in Napa, and producers and growers united against him. The handful of producers in the Rutherford AVA formed the Rutherford Dust Society to maintain the area's integrity. At the state-level Wine Institute, producers voted in committee to block Franzia's action, with even Ernest Gallo voting against Fred Franzia, his nephew. The Rutherford Dust Society petitioned the BATF, which then enjoined Franzia from selling the Rutherford-labeled wine. Franzia went to court, lost, and appealed, claiming the right to recoup the $42 million he had invested to purchase the brand. Andy Beckstoffer, a former president of the Rutherford Dust Society, described the incident as emblematic of a larger campaign for "real quality" and truth in advertising: "[Franzia] bought a whole bunch of little wineries, and markets them to look like they are individual little boutique wineries, when it's all the same fruit that comes from Ceres in the Central San Joaquin Valley."[47] The Napa producers' growers' campaign against him even drew support from the producers of Champagne in France. Meanwhile, Franzia rounded up some sixty-eight other California producers, including Korbel (which benefits from another legal loophole allowing it to call its sparkling wine *champagne*)—to an amicus curiae brief. Franzia won the first appeal. Four years later, however, the California State Supreme Court ruled for the Napa Valley Vintners.

"It's become a manhood issue," Franzia told the *Wall Street Journal* as he appealed the case to the U.S. Supreme Court.[48] In January 2006, the Supreme Court refused to hear the case. Thus six years of legal wrangling ended in upholding the California law from 2000 that stated that 75 percent of the grapes must come from the area if the brand has a geographic location in its name. Napa in the name means Napa in the bottle.

→>-<←

"Vote for L or go to Hell!" chanted Father John Brenkle in St. Helena in the spring of 2002. With a worldwide reputation for quality wine and its name now legally protected from dilution, Napa Valley was facing a new challenge: controversy over living conditions for vineyard workers. Father Brenkle, who had been a parish priest in St. Helena for twenty years, was campaigning for "the unseen," the Hispanic farm workers who had no political voice. Then more than seventy years old,

Brenkle had served on various committees to improve conditions for laborers in Napa Valley, obeying his vocation to care for "the least of God's brothers and sisters."[49]

At issue that spring was worker housing: there simply was not enough in this expensive valley. Particularly at the busy harvest time, many laborers had to commute long distances, camp out, or sleep on the porch of the local Catholic church. Because these conditions led to higher turnover, thereby increasing labor costs for producers, the Napa Valley Vintners Association voted to pool money to construct housing. The problem was finding a site for it. Joseph Phelps agreed to donate some land, but a county ballot initiative (Measure J) had established 40 and 160 acres as the minimum lot size for residential property in agricultural areas. Measure L, the local ballot initiative for which Father Brenkle was campaigning, would relax the local zoning regulations to allow construction on a smaller parcel.

Voters passed Measure L and the new law by 71 percent to 29. The housing was built on Phelps's land using funds from the state, the county, and the Napa Valley Vintners Association. Workers could now stay in a shared room with two or three others and receive three meals a day for $10. The only trouble was that the new facility had only 60 beds, bringing the total available within Napa County to around 300. Seasonal demand for labor brings 2,500 to 4,500 workers to the valley, which means that without more attention to the issue, Father Brenkle's porch will continue to be a busy place.

DISTRIBUTOR POLITICS

In the run-up to Prohibition, the forces advocating temperance were powerful enough to achieve their policy ends without the need for significant coalition partners, as chapter 2 shows. But in the wake of Repeal, with their power diminished, the Drys turned to efforts to influence state law and policy. In these campaigns the temperance advocates found strange bedfellows: the alcohol distributors.

The economist Bruce Yandle first referred to "bootleggers and Baptists" to describe the coupling of the bootleggers and the early temperance advocates,who agreed on prohibition but for different reasons, one economic and the other moral. Local bootleggers wanted to remove competition for their moonshine; the temperance advocates sought the abolition of alcohol sales based on their reading of the Bible (as well as their perceptions of the social harms caused by alcohol).[50] After Prohibition, the Drys' allies were the distributors instead of the bootleggers. A state has the power to set the rules on the transportation of alcohol within its boundaries. Many chose to enshrine a role for distributors in regulations that separate the businesses of alcohol production, distribution, and final sale. Thus a winery must sell to a distributor, who then sells to a retailer or a restaurant. Booz Allen Hamilton, the consulting firm, found the wine industry to have the most expensive distribution system of consumer packaged goods, with twice the margins of food distribution. "Regulation is intervening where the free-market economy would have driven a very different business solution," Larry Lowry, a senior partner at Booz Allen, told the *Wall Street Journal* in 1999.[51] How did this policy originate? How do quality producers challenge the institutional order? And what are the alternatives for consumers and small producers?

-+->-<+-

Chicago's Michigan Avenue has a Louis Vuitton store, a Niketown, and a Hershey's store. Many more stores within a few blocks boast "factory direct" items. Why is there no Gallo wine emporium bringing the wines of California directly to shoppers? It's not distance that explains it: there is no Gallo store in downtown San Francisco, either. Instead, it is the compromises struck at the time of Repeal, which have led to a complicated structure of laws controlling alcohol retailing in the United States. With respect to laws on wine sales, the fifty states resemble fifty sovereign nations.

Repeal resulted in a patchwork of state-level controls on distribution and final sale. Roosevelt ran on a repeal platform in 1932 with the argument that it would reinvigorate the economy. This argument, combined with the ineffectiveness of enforcement during Prohibition, led to the end of what Hoover had called the "noble experiment." However, many states still sought to maintain their dry status on moral principle. Thus the necessary support for Repeal at the federal level was built by making it optional—not federally mandated—at the state and local levels. Individual states retained the authority to decide whether, how, and where alcoholic beverages could be distributed.

Large sections of the country, including most of the Southern, Midwestern, and Mountain states and some of New England, stayed dry, while California, New York, Illinois, New Jersey, Massachusetts, Nevada, Oregon, Washington, and Wisconsin went "wet." The result was a broad array of systems for the production, distribution, and sale of alcoholic beverages. By the late 1930s most states had a repeal in place, but there were a few holdouts: Utah did not have a repeal on the books until 1959.[52]

The various state laws have some common features. All states require distributors and sellers of alcohol to hold a license. Applicants must submit to background examinations of finances and police records, just as wineries must undergo scrutiny from the federal authorities. Places of final sale are divided into two categories: on-premises consumption, such as restaurants and bars, and off-premises, such as liquor stores or specialty shops. Distribution and final sale must remain separate and distinct, a system meant to protect the retailer from being strong-armed by the distributor. Distributors cannot extend credit to the retailers or take ownership stakes in a retail operation. Gifts from a distributor to a retailer are limited to a value of less than $300 per year. Yet even within this system, distributors can exert power over retailers and restaurants, mainly by controlling payment terms and merchandise availability. Steve Boone, the cofounder of the Beverages & More retail chain, explains, "The tradeoff might be a position on the [restaurant] wine list in return for extended credit, or an eye-level position in a retail store in return for guaranteed availability."[53]

Whereas most states license distributors and retailers to provide alcohol to consumers, others states still retain control of distribution and sale themselves. Astonishingly for a country that espouses free-market principles, eighteen states, home to 28 percent of the U.S. population, still own the means of alcohol distribution or sale to their residents. Wine consumers in Park City, Utah, for example, must buy their wines at the windowless box known as State Liquor Store #34. The state runs thirty-six stores in the entire state, along with one hundred smaller "package agencies." In Iowa, operating a hybrid system since a degree of liberalization in 1986, taxes and fees on alcohol generated about 1 percent of the state's 2005 budget, or $77 million. In Pennsylvania, the Liquor Control Board is among the biggest wholesalers and retailers of wine and spirits in the country, retaining the exclusive right to sell wine to the state's 12 million residents.

In these "control" states, a Baptist-bootlegger coalition between state governments, social conservatives, and distributors provided the political foundation for a style of market governance that resembles that of the former Soviet Union more than the vision of Adam Smith. But the system endures largely because of the tax revenues it provides. In Pennsylvania, the Liquor Control Board generated $1.5 billion in sales and a profit of $350 million, which went back to the state treasury. While the Liquor Control Board argues that its purchasing power delivers competitive prices to consumers, the bevy of taxes blunts any such claim. A case of wine that the Liquor Control Board buys for $100 is subject to a 30 percent mark-up, a $10.80 "bottle handling" charge, and an 18 percent Johnstown Flood Tax (enacted in 1936 and never repealed), plus a "rounding up" to the nearest 99 cents and a local sales tax of 6 or 7 percent, depending on the county. The case might sell to the consumer for $166.42.

New York maintains odd regulations on distribution and final sale: no store selling food can also sell wine, and no wine-shop owner can own more than one store. Thus a national chain such as Trader Joe's must select one location that will sell wine (from a separate storefront adjacent to the grocery store), which partially explains the media frenzy and long lines outside the New York City store at the time of its opening in March 2006. Many other states and localities have "blue laws" regulating consumption, such as no consumption of liquor in public places, a ban on sales on Sundays or at night, or limits on the size of bottles available in bars. With the rise of the anti–drunk driving movement, the issue of liability lawsuits has motivated sellers, especially bar owners, to observe these laws strictly.[54]

As a result of these state laws, simply getting wines from producer to consumer can be difficult, not only because the laws themselves are obstructive but also because quirks in their provisions have given rise to peculiar distribution and retail practices. In the first few decades after Repeal, before good wine became widely available, distributors grew accustomed to the high and consistent sales volumes and standardized, branded products of beer and spirits. During that period, wine was sold by the jug and fit relatively easily into the distribution framework. This was also a period of "fair trade" in California, which suppressed price competition and forced retailers to compete on the basis of service. In this situation, Gallo adopted creative marketing practices. Particularly within California, where Gallo could distribute its own wines, the Gallo sales staff trained retailers in display techniques such as creating enticing eye-level displays, using a feather duster, and offering suggestions for pairing food and wine.[55]

Consolidation among both retailers and distributors makes competition revolve around price and favors larger-volume wine producers. Although no distributor serves the whole country, a handful of distributors, such as Southern Wine and Spirits, Glazer's, Charmer, and National Wine and Spirits control an ever-greater market share through entry into new states and the acquisition of local rivals (see table 6). The Wine Institute estimates that there are now only 300

TABLE 6. BIG IN THE MIDDLE: WINE AND
SPIRITS DISTRIBUTORS

Company	Forbes 2005 Rank	Headquarters	Revenues (Billions of Dollars)
Southern Wine and Spirits	31	Florida	5.90
Glazer's	84	Texas	2.80
Sunbelt	176	New York	1.77
National	188	Georgia	1.65
Young's Market	209	California	1.50
Republic Beverage	227	Texas	1.38
Wirtz	279	Illinois	1.15
Peerless	309	New York	1.05

SOURCE: Shlomo Reifman and Samantha N. Wong, "America's Largest Private Companies," *Forbes*, November 11, 2005.

distributors, down from 10,000 in 1963. Founded in 1968, Southern has been the most aggressive consolidator, with an estimated $5.9 billion in revenue and a rank of 31 on the Forbes Private 500 List. The pattern of fewer, bigger distributors dovetails with the trend toward "big box" retail stores. Price competition is now permitted in many states, and the fair-trade laws that once prevailed in California look anachronistic. Today, more than half of wine sales occur in supermarkets, including warehouse stores such as Sam's Club and Costco, which together account for about a third of the wine sold in the United States.

-+>-<+-

How do the changes in the distribution and retail structure affect producers? With fewer distributors in the middle, a large number of dispersed retailers, and an expanding number of U.S. wineries—now more than 5,300, according to *Wine Business Monthly*—the asymmetry in the market presents a significant obstacle for small producers. Boutique wineries have two ways to sell their wines: they can either use a distributor or sell to the consumer directly from the winery. However, distributors can be wary of taking on a small producer because supplies can be limited and quality can vary from vintage to vintage. As a result, the small high-quality producers often try to sell their entire production through a mailing list directly to consumers, a practice that allows them to charge the retail price at the winery door and greatly expand their profit margin. (On a case of wine with a retail price of $195, for example, the winery will make about $30 profit after the distributor and retailer have taken their cuts—about $40 and $55, respectively. The same wine sold at the same price direct to the consumer yields a profit of approximately $115, taking into account the additional costs to the winery of selling directly to consumers.) Direct sales also allow boutique winery owners to manage distribution, ensuring that a consumer who wants a quality product can get it and encouraging word-of-mouth promotion. The owner of a small winery in Sonoma told me why she sells directly to consumers and restaurants, bypassing shops: "The case of wine in a restaurant may be ordered for twelve tables. In a shop, one person could buy the whole case. This way more people get to try our wines."

Selling wine directly to consumers has drawbacks. Either the consumers must come to the winery to collect the wine or the winery must ship it to them, a situation that effectively limits the market. Before 2005, direct shipping was legal in less than half of the fifty states. Granted, some big states such as California and Illinois were included, but other large states, including New York, Florida, Pennsylvania, and Texas were not. Moreover, success in selling directly to consumers depends on an established reputation and favorable reviews from critics. Thus only the rare winery can sell its entire production through a mailing list.

What small winery owners must do instead is find a distributor in every state where they want to sell their wine The case of Richard and Alis Arrowood in Sonoma is illustrative of the challenges. Dick Arrowood was a successful winemaker whose wine won critical and popular approval during his many years at Chateau St. Jean. After the winery changed hands, a growing restlessness led Arrowood to start his own winery in Sonoma in 1986. His name recognition and experience gave him an advantage, as loyal customers were willing to follow him to his new winery. In pricing his wines, Arrowood admitted to using the "SWAG method" or "scientific wild-ass guess" (an approach not recommended for small-business owners but surprisingly common among boutique winery owners). He decided to compete in the ultrapremium category, pricing his wine at about $25 retail.[56]

Following a pattern common in small wineries, the founding couple divided the workload. Dick made the wines, and Alis sold them. In the first year of production, the couple found life easy because Southern Wine and Spirits committed to buy their entire 4,000-case production. Southern was the distributor for Chateau St. Jean and wanted to maintain good ties with Arrowood. But Alis Arrowood found that the wines were not appearing in the shops and restaurants where she wanted them. The distributor explained that Arrowood was a fine wine, but with such a small production volume, the sales staff was reluctant to push the wine for fear that a repeat order would go unfilled. Southern was more firmly behind other wines that had bigger production volumes and would not be likely to disappoint restaurants and shops with availability problems. So, under the terms of their contract, the Arrowoods purchased back the remaining inventory and started to sell it themselves.

Selling the product was a grueling task, and in the early years Alis Arrowood was on the road twenty-six weeks of the year. She went to trade shows and cultivated relationships with distributors and key retailers and restaurant owners around the country, focusing on the largest markets. On a typical sales trip, Alis would stop at shops and restaurants that sold her wines, offer a tasting, and provide talking points that would help the staff promote the wines. She gave talks at "vintner dinners" at clubs and restaurants, in which diners paid for a meal and she enthusiastically presented her wines. (The focused tastings of a dinner or small-group setting are key selling opportunities for a small winery.) Then she would repeat the program somewhere else the next day.

The Arrowoods sold their winery in 1999 to Robert Mondavi (which in turn was purchased by a bigger firm in 2004), but today's small producers face the same challenges in navigating the distributor channel. Another small, high-end producer from Napa said that the whimsical name of his winery cut against the grain of wine culture, so he had to rely on strategic tastings, particularly in the early years. When in New York, he wines and dines the three sales representatives from his distributor to help them get to know and remember his product line.[57] Although the Internet has created new opportunities for small producers to sell directly to consumers, some small California producers still load their cars with wine and drive all over the state to hold tastings.

As a response to this disadvantage of size, and also in reaction to their perceived marginalization in the Wine Institute, small producers formed the Family Winemakers of California in 1991. The organization has more than three hundred members, who pay dues in proportion to their production volume. The association not only gives smaller producers a voice in the California state legislature, but it also helps improve distributor relations and boost sales. Because tasting is a key selling strategy for small, high-quality producers, the association holds an annual two-day tasting in San Francisco. The event is well attended by restaurateurs, retailers, and writers.

To simplify the logistics of storage and shipping, some small producers in Napa Valley formed the Wine Service Co-op in 1970. Joseph
Phelps helped create the 200,000-square-foot facility, and thirty-six
small and mid-sized wineries participate. Dan Duckhorn, a maker of
Merlot, among other wines, said, "We all love that place, because after
our wine is bottled, it goes there for bottle aging and storage, and is
shipped out from there. We never see it or touch it again.... That
mechanical part is left to the cooperative or others, and it helps us
focus."[58] This solution facilitates selling directly to consumers.

Bigger producers can attract distributors with economies of scale
and corporate tactics. Beringer is one of the most business-oriented
wineries in Napa Valley, having been owned variously by Nestlé, a private equity group, a publicly traded company, and, since 2002, a unit
of Foster's, the Australian beer and wine producer. Mike Moone, CEO
at Beringer in the 1980s and previously at Procter and Gamble,
described the tactics he employed during his tenure. Beringer was run
as a business. He hired a sales team with backgrounds ranging from
United States military service to brand management at Clorox or Procter and Gamble. Moone said that "achievement far outweighed wine
knowledge" among his salespeople. And in case the large volumes and
a crack sales team to move the pallets were not sufficient to attract the
attention of distributors, Moone brought his national distributors to
Napa once a year for a multiday golf outing at the Silverado Country
Club in Napa.[59]

Small wineries mostly cannot compete on this scale, but there is an
increasing number of tactics they can use to attract attention from distributors. Over the past decade, midsized wineries have teamed with
distributors and importers for marketing campaigns. Cakebread Cellars of Rutherford, producer of the most popular restaurant wine in
2005, has engaged the New York–based distributor Kobrand to undertake its national marketing campaign. Wine importers and brand
builders such as W. J. Deutsch & Sons and Terlato Wine Group also
offer marketing services for domestic wineries. This is such a growth
area that Michael Mondavi, the former CEO of Robert Mondavi, has
started a company called Folio that performs exactly these services.[60]

Parallel to the consolidation of distributors has been the rise of
niche distributors with a smaller and often more exciting portfolio.
Many operate in the competitive markets. Examples include the Henry
Wine Group in California and Michael Skurnik, Winebow, VOS Selections, and Polaner in New York.

Playing Hardball

Despite their already-dominant position in the market, in the mid-1990s the distributors initiated a campaign aimed to reinforce their power: the attempt to lobby states to classify out-of-state shipments of wine as a felony. Putting wine shipments on a par with murder and invoking the rhetoric of protecting children, distributors claimed that without stronger control over distribution, minors would have easy access to alcohol. Moreover, direct sales by out-of-state producers, which bypass distributors, also bring little or no tax revenue to states and counties. The distributors have tried to position themselves as the allies of the states, collectors of revenue and protectors of minors.

Among the distributors, Southern Wine and Spirits has arguably been playing hardest to win, a strategy which fueled a rapid rise in the company's profits and influence. In two lengthy and hard-hitting stories on Southern in October 1999, the *Wall Street Journal* followed the trail of money and influence that led to the enactment of the felony laws.[61] They traced one strand to a flyer offering direct shipment of wine from a California wine retailer to Florida consumers, on which the Southern executive Mel Dick had written his colleague Wayne Chaplin a note: "Is there any way to stop this?" The *Journal* writers observed that Southern subsequently unleashed a "torrent" of lobbying in Talla-hassee (making $60,000 in contributions to legislators), and within two years the legislature had put the felony law on the books (against the wishes of the state attorney general). A felony conviction would be partic-ularly damaging for winery owners, as it would mean revocation of their federal winery license.

On the one hand, Southern seems to be a story of successful American corporation. Founded in 1968, the company capitalized on consumers' growing interest in fine wine and dining and invested in staff training, working with wineries such as Robert Mondavi in an education program and assembling a strong portfolio of wines. Its managers developed and executed an exceptionally successful growth strategy that either crushed or acquired the competition. Even today, with more than $6 billion in revenue after its dramatic entry into the New York market, the company continues to hire and acquire top talent. It invests heavily in its infrastruc-ture, which includes a climate-controlled warehouse in Nevada that is so highly mechanized that no human ever has to touch a bottle.

Southern's margins are high, and the executives have fought tooth and nail to protect them. The *Journal* quotes Tom Shelton, the CEO of

Joseph Phelps, as saying that "their warehouses and trucks are worth something," but not the markups being charged. The story also cites the example of a Florida entrepreneur who got a distributor license simply to facilitate the importation of cult wine from California for Florida wine consumers. But the Florida Division of Alcohol Beverages and Tobacco charged the entrepreneur with failing to comply with a 1996 law stating that distributors must carry a minimum inventory. He is now out of business. Southern was behind the 1996 law to thwart small-scale competitors.

In Nevada, Southern has grown from nothing in 1970 to be the top player in providing wine to the state's dining and entertainment industry, which includes the hotels of Las Vegas. In a fascinating article in *Wine & Spirits* magazine, Jordan Mackay calls Southern the "Microsoft of the Nevada wine world (and just as powerful in many other states)," a dominant business position that doesn't always generate friends. He comments that Southern's "sins, in the eyes of those who would denigrate it, are typical of the complaints one hears of the juggernauts in any business: They have too much power, enabling them to squelch competition that is necessary for a healthy market. They dictate terms to customers instead of the other way around. They, rather than the market, dictate prices." However, there may be more than sharp elbows in play in Nevada. MGM's Seablue restaurant opened in 2004 with almost half its inventory of wines purchased from NWA, another distributor. The Seablue wine director, Mackay reports, "got a call that his new Mercedes convertible had been stolen and found torched in the desert."[62]

The distributors also flex their muscles through political lobbying. Southern made $278,000 worth of campaign contributions in the 2004 Congressional election cycle, according to the Center for Responsive Politics. It distributed its contributions evenly between Democrats and Republicans. The Wine and Spirits Wholesalers Association (WSWA) gave more than twice that amount, with donations skewed toward incumbent Republicans. The WSWA was among a group of top donors in the 2000 presidential cycle.[63] And in Michigan, the distributors lavished Caribbean trips on legislators and their spouses in the middle of winter. These sums may seem small, but Warren Buffett, a proponent of campaign-finance reform, has called political influence "the world's most underpriced commodity." The *Detroit Free Press* ran a series of articles by Jennifer Dixon on the influence of distributors and concluded, among other things, that the price of beer and wine was higher in Michigan than in surrounding states because distributors used political donations to gain influence and limit competition.[64] In Ohio, where the state mandates that wholesalers add a minimum markup of 33.3 percent to wine prices, the *Columbus Dispatch* reports that the Wholesale Beer and Wine Association of Ohio donated $1.16 million to politicians and political parties between 2001 and 2005.[65]

Several states grant exclusive licenses to distributors under what are known as "franchise laws." For example, in the state of Georgia, when a winery selects a distributor, the winery cannot terminate the relationship, regardless of the performance of the distributor. One prominent winemaker was working with a small distributor that was then acquired by one of the top national firms. The Napa winemaker refused to place his wines with this company, but Georgia law prevented him from changing. His only option was to withdraw his wines from sale in Georgia. After a statutory period of four years, he would be allowed to re-enter the state with a new distributor. The catch? The big distributor is holding some of his cases in its warehouse, preventing him from applying for reentry to the state. "We budget for legal battles. At the beginning there was no line item for legal. Now with success, legal has crept into the budget," he said. This type of activity is tantamount to "regulatory abuse" in the eyes of the quality wine producers, as one testified before Congress.[66]

-+>-<+-

Many small-scale wine producers have tried to end their reliance on powerful distributors. In 1999 the head of the Napa Valley Vintners Association proposed using the Internet to boost direct sales. But distributors objected, arguing that the Internet would spur underage drinking in the absence of a "face-to-face" transaction at a shop. To address these claims, he proposed a system of checking the drivers' licenses of the buyers. He did not favor doorstep delivery to residences in any case because, in his words, "The last thing I want is a $1,200 case of wine sitting on someone's doorstep in Florida in 90 degree heat."[67] The reluctance of Congress to act in regard to wine policy made it a matter for the courts. On the one hand, free traders—consumer groups and small wineries—pointed to the interstate commerce clause of the Constitution to justify their claim. On the other hand, an alliance akin to the "Baptists and bootleggers," pairing social conservatives with economic protectionists, pointed to a state's right under the Twenty-first Amendment to regulate alcohol distribution and sale, which, they argued, took precedence over the commerce clause. For

federalist justices—proponents of states' rights over federal authority—
the case divided their loyalties between free trade and states' rights.

Odd alliances emerged among the free traders to shepherd cases
through the district courts in the hope of generating conflicting rulings,
which would make it more likely that the Supreme Court would hear
the case and rule definitively on the issue—although the outcome of a
Supreme Court decision was far from certain. The libertarian Institute
for Justice, the Coalition for Free Trade, and Free the Grapes engaged in
what sociologists and practitioners of law call "forum shopping" as
cases came before the courts in six states. Many consumers, particularly
in small states, argue that the entrenched position of distributors
restricts their access to wines, particularly high-quality wines from boutique producers. The strange bedfellows of the free-trade litigation team
targeted eight states which had laws that allowed in-state shipments of
wine directly to residents while prohibiting out-of-state shipments. One
was New York, the nation's second largest wine market, and also the
home of many major media outlets, whose influence is decisive in the
court of public opinion. The 250 wine producers in New York State, for
example, could ship to New York residents, but the producers of Virginia or California could not; the free traders argued that this situation
violated the commerce clause. Clint Bolick, a litigator for the free
traders, invoked not only the commerce clause but also the "privileges
and immunities clause" of the Fourteenth Amendment.[68] He used this
clause to suggest that residents of one state should not be able to enjoy
privileges that residents of another cannot. The free traders' arguments
carried the day in New York.

When the Supreme Court decided to hear cases from Michigan and
New York, the trial turned into a battle royal. The free traders retained
Kenneth Starr (celebrated in conservative circles for his role as independent counsel investigating President Bill Clinton) as co-counsel. The
distributors retained Robert Bork, the first Supreme Court nominee
ever to be rejected for his (conservative) political views rather than
simply on the basis of qualifications. Seven economists, including the
Nobel Prize winners George Akerlof and Daniel McFadden, coau-
thored a friend of the court brief in support of the free traders.

On May 16, 2005, the Supreme Court ruled for the wineries and the
consumers and against the distributors in a 5–4 decision. "The current
patchwork of laws," wrote Justice Anthony Kennedy in the majority
opinion, was "essentially the product of an ongoing, low-level trade
war." He continued that although the Twenty-first Amendment

granted wide powers to the states, "state regulation of alcohol is limited by the nondiscrimination principle of the Commerce Clause."
Underscoring the odd pattern of alliances on this issue, the decision
was opposed by Chief Justice William Rehnquist and Justices Clarence
Thomas, Sandra Day O'Connor, and John Paul Stevens. In his dissent-
ing opinion, Justice Thomas wrote that the Twenty-first Amendment
"took those policy choices away from judges and returned them to the
states."

In fact, the ruling did return the prerogative to the states, where legislators and governors had to decide either to alter state laws to provide equal access for wineries in-state and out of state, or shut down
direct-to-consumer shipments altogether. In New York, Governor
Pataki quickly embraced liberalization, touting the opportunities for
New York wineries to ship wine to many other states and neglecting
the possibility that New York residents who had been making do with
New York State wines might opt for other choices. In a show of
bravura when he signed the bill into law at a winery in the Finger
Lakes on July 13, Pataki said, "I have no doubt that the Finger Lakes
can certainly match, maybe even surpass" California's famed Napa
Valley someday. He added: "It is an excellent standard to shoot for but
I don't see any reason why we can't achieve that."[69] In Michigan, after
a protracted lobbying struggle that galvanized the state's forty-two
wineries and consumers to take on the wholesalers, the state liberalized
its laws on shipping in early 2006. Florida, Texas, and many other
states that had been closed to out-of-state shipments have opened up
since the Supreme Court decision.

Possibly more meaningful for consumers, but less sensational, is the
case of *Costco Wholesale Corp v. Hoen,* in the U.S. District Court for
the Western District of Washington. Whereas the cases brought before
the U.S. Supreme Court mainly affect high-end wines, as the costs of
interstate shipping are high (some wineries charge $65 to ship a case
across the country), the *Costco* case could affect wines at all price
points. Essentially, it takes the equality principle that the Supreme
Court laid down in May 2005, stipulating that states cannot treat in-
state shipments differently from out-of-state shipments, and applies it
to distributors. Many states, including Washington, where Costco is
based, permit wineries within a state to bypass distributors for delivery
to retailers. But wineries based in other states are not allowed to sell to
retailers directly. The District Court ruled in Costco's favor in April

2006. The defendants, including the Washington Beer and Wine Wholesalers Association, have appealed.

For an illustration of how this could affect prices, consider Bronco Wine Company, owned by Fred Franzia, the fourth largest wine producer in the United States. The company entered into an exclusive agreement with the national retailer Trader Joe's to sell a wine (known as Two Buck Chuck) under its Charles Shaw label for $2 retail. However, that price applies only in California, where Bronco can act as its own distributor, selling directly to Trader Joe's. In other states, where Bronco must pass its inventory through distributors before it reaches Trader Joe's, the wine effectively becomes "three buck Chuck" or even "four buck Chuck." While such markups may not seem large in absolute terms, the percentage difference is very high. If wineries could distribute directly to retailers, prices could drop considerably, particularly at the low end.

Lower prices for wine would certainly contribute to the strong growth in wine consumption. Because about one-third of Americans do not drink any alcohol, per capita consumption rates have lagged behind those of other countries. According to a study undertaken by the French trade group Vinexpo, however, the United States will be the largest consumer of wine by 2008, surpassing France and Italy. A July 2005 Gallup poll showed that Americans preferred wine over beer for the first time in their polling. King James and Thomas Jefferson would be proud.

CHAPTER 5

Who Controls Your Palate?

In this era of globalization, is wine becoming homogeneous? As consolidation has swept the industry, giving rise to more corporate brands, some argue that consumers are doomed to an era in which brand equals bland. Further, some critics have become so powerful that wine producers from around the world make wines explicitly to satisfy their palates. Does the rise of corporations and critics mean the end of diversity in wine?

→>−<+−

The cases of Yellow Tail were stacked to twice my height. Was I in a distributor's warehouse? No, I was in Sam's Wine and Spirits in Chicago. The store is a wine lover's paradise, offering almost ten thousand different wines in a warehouse that feels as big as a Boeing assembly plant. Before reaching the rows of limited-production wines, I had to walk by stacked cases of lower-end wines. The biggest display was of Yellow Tail, an Australian wine with a distinctive marsupial logo. It looked as if it had been lowered in by crane and the shipping container removed.

Yellow Tail is the 900-pound wallaby that has leapt into the American wine business. Australian wine sales have gained a huge market share in the United States: in 1994, sales were small, but ten years later Australia provided more wine to the United States than any other exporting nation, including France and Italy. Yellow Tail epitomizes this rapid rise. In its first year, 2001, it sold an already large quantity, 250,000 cases; in 2005, it sold 8.6 million cases. Total imports of

Figure 5. Casella Winery, Griffith, New South Wales, the home of Yellow Tail. With 60 million liters of storage capacity and a bottling line that can handle 65,000 bottles an hour, Yellow Tail is on its way to providing more wine to the American market than all of France. Courtesy Casella Winery.

French wine to the U.S. in 2005 were 10.5 million cases. The Yellow Tail brand was competitive with the entire output of France.

W. J. Deutsch and Sons, Yellow Tail's North American importer, based in White Plains, New York, owns half of the rights to Yellow Tail in North America, with the other half belonging to the wine's producers, the Casella family.[1] Bill Deutsch, whose company has ridden the wave of Yellow Tail to become one of the top five wine marketers in America, told me that consistency is important: "One of the reasons for success of the brand is that case one tasted the same as case one million."[2] John Casella has elaborated on his production style in an interview on Grape Radio, saying that he wanted to "tailor it to the market," aiming to make it "much friendlier" than some "awful" Italian wine he had tasted in his youth. Specifically, he said, "We need to tone the tannin back, we need to soften it, and we don't want excess acidity for ordinary drinkers. You really want something that is soft, fruity, with a great aftertaste."[3] The wine also has a high level of residual sugar, which gives it a notice-able sweetness.

The brand started with just two wines, a Chardonnay and a Shiraz. Each came in two sizes, a standard bottle of 750 mL and one of 1.5 liters.

That generated just four inventory numbers and product bar codes. For distributors and large retailers, these categories were easy to understand: white, red, small, and big. American consumers also found Yellow Tail easy to understand, with its English-language name, the readily recognizable wallaby on the label, and the name written in lowercase and placed in brackets, making it look informal and vaguely techie. With a retail price of $6, those four bar codes were scanned at a lot of registers. The huge demand meant that back in Australia, John Casella had to hire more winemakers, build a massive winery (figure 5), and find more grapes. To maintain the consistency of the brand, the winery also had to intervene in the winemaking process to override the influence of *terroir*.

-+->-<+-

Australia had lots of grapes to offer. Until 2004, the government subsidized vineyard plantings, giving rise to a mountain of grapes. Many of the Australian growing areas experienced stable growing conditions, without the threat of rain at harvest that haunts Burgundy and Bordeaux every September. The Australian growers do not have prohibitions on irrigation in the vineyard, as the appellation growers do, so they can further compensate for the vagaries of weather and grow in arid regions. The domestic market of 20 million inhabitants was not enough to absorb it all. Australia had become a provider of wine to the world.

Marketing and Australian wine have a long history, with the first plantings dating from the nineteenth century. The writer James Halliday recounts that in 1954 David Wynn, a pioneer in Australian wine making, was actively marketing the wines of Coonawarra, in South Australia. Wynn said: "My prime aim is an extensive advertising campaign in Melbourne to make Coonawarra famous. People, when thinking of Claret, would then naturally think of Coonawarra." He succeeded, Halliday writes, "beyond his wildest expectations," as Coonawarra Cabernet Sauvignon developed a strong reputation.[4] Starting in the 1980s, the Australian Wine and Brandy Corporation, an institution funded by growers and the government, ran promotional campaigns— and the brand was Australia itself. Building on this tradition for its marketing, in a series of print and outdoor advertisements, William Deutsch spent an estimated $24 million on advertising the brand in 2006.[5]

Initially, however, Australia sent only its worst wine abroad. The situation changed in the 1980s, as plantings expanded and the industry began to focus on the export markets. The Australian Wine and Brandy Corporation introduced minimum quality standards for exported wines.

With their resulting high quality and low price, Australian wines undercut many competitors in the world market and rapidly gained market
share. In 1970 a scant 4,000 cases of wine were exported to the United
States. That quantity increased by 1980 to 44,000 cases—still just 0.1
percent of U.S. wine imports. By 1990, 491,000 cases were imported,
accounting for 1.7 percent market share. And by 2004, Australian
imports exceeded 20 million cases, representing more than 25 percent of
U.S. wine imports.

-+->-<-+-

Globalization in the wine industry has been a boon for the American
consumer. Good, affordable wine has poured into the United States
from Australia and other countries. Worldwide, producers are making
more wine than is consumed. Producer pain spells consumer gain, as it
allows buyers to pick and choose.

But the effect of competition from the Southern Hemisphere and
places like Spain and Italy on wine producers in France—and America
to a certain extent—has been significant. As figure 6 shows, not only
did Australia surpass France in total exports to America in 2002 and
Italy in 2005 to become the largest exporter of wine to the U.S. market,
but the imported wine accounts for an increasingly large share of the
total U.S. market: in 2005 it accounted for 27 percent of the wine
Americans drank, more than double its market share in 1990. As
Frank Prial has noted, a hard-hitting report in April 2006 from Silicon
Valley Bank admonished American wine producers in California's Central Valley for ceding ground to affordable wines from overseas. "Are
American vintners starting to look like Detroit in the 70's, when gas
prices soared and automakers kept putting out big gas guzzlers?" the
report wondered. Following the success of Yellow Tail and fruit-forward Pinot Grigio from Italy, the report cautioned that "the U.S. will
no longer be able to ignore the depth of the world glut (which keeps
import prices low), or the high cost of American production for lower
price-point wines." The report cited production costs for some foreign
wine regions as being one-third of those of the Central Valley.[6]

Those are harsh words for an industry that has managed thus far to
find a market for a vast quantity of low-priced wine. The charismatic
Fred Franzia has proclaimed that "no bottle of wine is worth more
than $10 in my opinion."[7] His portfolio includes Two Buck Chuck,
which sells 5 million cases a year. This was a wine for everyday drinking, but it was not marketed as a cheap jug wine: it came in a standard-

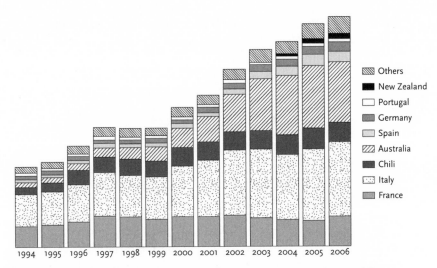

Figure 6. U.S. wine imports by country of origin, 1994–2005. Source: *The U.S. Wine Market: Impact Databank, Review, and Forecast* (New York: M. Shanken Communications, 2005).

sized bottle with a cork. Shoppers at Trader Joe's loaded it ten cases at a time into their SUVs. Two Buck Chuck may have done more for popularizing wine than either the *60 Minutes* report on the health benefits of red wine or the movie *Sideways.* Sales of inexpensive wine have also expanded through the use of the increasingly popular three-liter bag-in-a-box packaging, which has earned praise from some wine writers because it retards oxidation.

American producers had long been content with satisfying the domestic market. Indeed, it took a kick start with federal funds to induce them to start exporting. In 1985 Congress passed the Wine Equity Act, which made wine eligible for export subsidies. This Matching Promotion Program (MPP) matched federal funds to winery funds to promote export. Patrick Campbell of Laurel Glen in Sonoma testified to the value of this program before Congress in 1993: "We got started early; we doggedly pursued foreign opportunities, participated in Vinexpo, visited Europe at least yearly, and sponsored generic advertising programs for American wines in several countries. None of this would have been possible without MPP funds."[8] The funds amounted to as much as $4.83 million, or 13.8 percent of the $35 million total exports in 1986, but trailed off after 1994, while exports increased.

TABLE 7. FRENCH WINE EXPORTS TO THE
UNITED STATES, 2001–2005

Year	Value of Wine (Millions of Euros)
2001	854,305
2002	937,863
2003	955,968
2004	824,239
2005	875,875

NOTE: Includes still and sparkling wines. SOURCE: French Trade Office, New York.

In the early days, exports were more about reputation than about profit, as the Napa vintner Dan Duckhorn said: "I think it's about . . . credibility. . . . When we started out our goal was to emulate some of the first growths and second growths of Bordeaux, and credibility was a part of that, and worldwide recognition is a part of that."[9] Today U.S. wine exports also account for serious money: they reached $794 million in 2004, although they fell to $660 million in 2005. To put these figures in perspective, in 2002 the U.S. exported $550 million, which accounted for about 4 percent of global wine exports. French exports were roughly ten times that figure.

If Silicon Valley Bank analysts take a dim view of the California wine industry, what would they think of the troubled French wine industry? Most likely they would call for a consolidation of an industry that employs 300,000 people and for bolstering exports. France has traditionally been the world's leading wine exporter by value. Between 1994 and 1998 exports rose from €3.3 billion to €5.8 billion. But since then the figure has remained between €5.4 billion and €5.9 billion, while other countries have been increasing exports sharply.[10] This erosion of foreign market share, combined with declining domestic consumption, explains how French appellation wine ended up being distilled into ethanol for the first time in 2005.

French winemakers take it on the chin when France ruffles diplomatic feathers. Because wine and French identity are closely intertwined, wine often is the object of foreign boycotts (see table 7). When French security agents blew up the Greenpeace ship *Rainbow Warrior* in New Zealand in the 1980s, when the French conducted nuclear tests in the South Pacific, and when Dominique de Villepin opposed Colin Powell at the United Nations over the invasion of Iraq, French wine ended up in the gutters as consumers expressed their disgust. (American wines have not yet wrested the dubious distinction from McDonald's and Coca-Cola of being the targets of anti-American protests.) While consumer boycotts and the wholesale discarding of products may have a whiff of grandstanding or the absurd, two Stanford economists have estimated that the 2003 diplomatic stand-off cost the French wine industry $124 million.[11]

With high taxes and labor pushing up costs, bankers or management consultants might advise France to take the high road and leave the production of bulk wine to low-cost producers in Chile, Argentina, Australia, and South Africa. The whirling vortex of cute and clear English-language labels and large marketing budgets has largely passed over France. French wine in America has often been marketed—if at all—on the strength of its tradition and prestige. That strategy works at the higher price points, but not for consumers seeking fun and affordable bottles. Abandoning price-competitive wines, as a management consultant might advise, would ignore the difficulties of many *vignerons*. Instead, the French winemakers are rising to meet the challenge.

The downturn in exports to the United States has made some French producers refocus their efforts. The proposed reforms of EU wine policy also provide carrots and sticks. Chamarré, for example, is a new brand from the Languedoc, created for export to the United Kingdom and the United States, from a cooperative that unites some 15,000 producers. Some appellation wines from Bordeaux are now being marketed with the grape varieties on the label, thus competing head to head with New World wines. In the United States, the French wine promotion authority Sopexa launched a promotional campaign in 2006 led by Sheri Sauter, who holds the prestigious title of Master of Wine. Sauter, a thirty-year-old American who does not speak French, selected forty affordable wines (such as a Bordeaux aged in American oak and a Pinot Noir from the Languedoc) with accessible labels, and English names and nontraditional packaging, such as a single-serving Champagne "mini" to drink straight from the bottle with a straw or the "French rabbit," which comes in a one-liter box. While overall French wine exports rallied slightly from 2005 to 2006, sales of these brands were up 20 percent.

Even though Champagne has built some of the most successful brands in the world, the use of brand names has not spread to other French wines—until recently. The *négociant* Mouton-Cadet has had some success, thanks to a halo effect from its *grand vin*. The brand Fat Bastard (co-owned by Peter Click, an American importer, and Gabriel Meffre, a strong exporter based in the Rhône) sells 500,000 cases. Some other brands from *négociants* such as Barton and Guestier, and Boisset have succeeded. Even American producers are starting to make branded wines in France, including Gallo's Red Bicyclette and Brown-Forman's Gala Rouge. But variation from one vintage to another, the high cost of land and labor, and the small size of landholdings have thus far worked against the creation of brands in France. Capital, including French capital, has flown elsewhere.

-+>-<+-

One of the paradoxes of this globalized era is that although the humble French *vigneron* has suffered of late, savvy French corporations have been adventurous and acquisitive overseas. French wine companies have properties in China, Chile, California, Australia, New Zealand, and many other places. Pernod-Ricard, one of the biggest drinks companies in the world, owns successful brands in Australia and New Zealand. LVMH owns wineries on five continents, and many Bordelais as well as many Champagne houses own properties in the United States. The Drouhin family of Burgundy, for example, has a significant winery in Oregon. In Argentina, several members of the French wine industry, including LVMH, the d'Aulan family of Sansonnet in Bordeaux, Jacques and Francois Lurton (the sons of André Lurton), and the Bordelais involved in a vast project called Clos de los Siete, have bought up properties. Furthermore, coopers such as Seguin Moreau and Taransaud have exported French oak barrels around the world.

Although not as heavily consolidated as the soft-drink and tobacco industries, wine production worldwide has consolidated rapidly in the past five years. The American company Constellation has been highly acquisitive, bagging Robert Mondavi and Canada's Vincor, among others. The privately held E. & J. Gallo has made several acquisitions as well as creating several new brands, such as Red Bicyclette from the Languedoc. Pernod-Ricard seized the biggest recent prize, Allied Domecq, but divested itself of some wine holdings to avoid antitrust complications.

All of these corporations regard wine as a brand: Constellation's corporate tag line is in fact "Building stellar brands." A brand manager oversees each label and is expected to deliver growth. Many of these companies are publicly traded and have to show results to their shareholders. Although sales of wine, particularly premium wine, have been growing, these global drinks companies often bundle together diverse holdings (see table 8) to balance the fluctuations of the wine business, which eventually drove Coca-Cola out of the industry.

This increasing consolidation has many implications. One is the cost savings made possible by economies of scale. Making several wines under one winery roof can reduce fixed costs. For example, when Constellation acquired the Blackstone Winery, then producing 400,000 cases annually, the company was able to save $800,000 a year because Constellation could save $2 per case on bottles. Similarly, marketing costs per brand can decrease thanks to larger heft in purchasing advertisements.

But do consumers pay a price for the bulking up of the wine industry? And how do producers achieve the consistency that Bill Deutsch wants in Yellow Tail? I found part of the answer in Paris.

—>—<—

The slight man at the lectern was bespectacled and balding and had a large gray moustache. I was at a wine trade show in Paris and checked his name and affiliation in the program: Bertrand Garrigues, CEO of Lamothe-Abiet, a subsidiary of Novozymes. Novozymes, the Danish biotech company? Sure enough. But what was he doing at a wine trade show?

The first slide of Garrigues's PowerPoint presentation showed two ways to make wine (each advocated by different factions; see chapter 3). The first was to start with the vineyard and make the wine that the vineyard naturally produced. The second and more expedient was to start with consumer demand and make a wine to suit it. How was Garrigues proposing to arrive at this consumer-friendly wine? Through enzymes—protein molecules that catalyze chemical reactions and can alter the character of the wine.

While most consumers know about oak influence in wine, and some wine buffs understand the effects of malolactic fermentation, the role of enzymes and yeasts is largely overlooked in consumer publications. Jamie Goode observes in *The Science of Wine* that "of the estimated 1,000 or so volatile flavor compounds in wine, at least 400 are produced by yeast."[12] In traditional wine making, when the grapes are crushed, the sugars of the flesh come in contact with the naturally occurring yeasts on the skins. As the yeasts consume the sugars, the fermentation process begins, creating alcohol. This type of "spontaneous" or "wild yeast" fermentation is regarded with nostalgia and even hostility in some wine-making circles (mostly in the New World, and mostly by corporations).

TABLE 8. THE BIGGEST WINE FIRMS AND THEIR BRANDS, JUNE 2006

Firm (HQ)	Wine Sales (Millions of 9-Liter Cases)	Market Capitalization	Representative Wine Brands	Select Other Holdings and Products
Constellation Brands (Fairport, NY)	93 worldwide; 54 U.S.	$5.5 billion ($4.6 billion revenue)	Almaden, Inglenook, Vendange, Talus, Franciscan, Robert Mondavi, Woodbridge, Ravenswood, Simi, Estancia, Covey Run, Manischewitz, Paul Masson, Kim Crawford, Hogue, Veramonte, Banrock Station, Cook's	Arbor Mist, Paul Masson; U.S. brand owner for Corona, Negra Modelo, St. Pauli Girl
E. & J. Gallo (Modesto, CA)	75	Privately held	Gallo labels, Mirassou, Barefoot Cellars, Ecco Domani (Italy), Red Bicyclette (France)	E&J brandy
The Wine Group (San Francisco)	42	Privately held	Corbett Canyon, Foxhorn, Mogen David Kosher, Franzia	—
Bronco Wine (Ceres, CA)	20	Privately held	Charles Shaw, Forestville, Estrella, Montpellier, Grand Cru, Silver Ridge, Rutherford Vintners, Hacienda, Fox Hollow, Harlow Ridge	—
Fosters Wine Group (Victoria, Australia)	17	Publicly traded	U.S.: Beringer, Etude, Stags' Leap, St. Clement, Chateau St. Jean, Chateau Souverain, Asti; Australia: Penfolds	Foster's, Victoria Bitter, Karloff, Strongbow
Diageo (London)	5	$48 billion ($13 billion in revenue)	Beaulieu Vineyards, Sterling Vineyards, Blossom Hill, Chalone, Sagelands, Edna Valley, Acacia, Canoe Ridge, Echelon, Provenance, Bodegas Norton, Barton & Guestier (importer)	Smirnoff, Johnnie Walker, J&B, Bailey's Irish Cream, Captain Morgan, Cuervo, Tanqueray, Ciroc, Guinness, Bass, Crown Royal

Company	Case sales (millions)	Revenue	Wine brands	Other brands
Trinchero Family Estates (St. Helena, CA)	9.3	Privately held	Sutter Home, Trinchero, Fre, Montevina, Folie à Deux	—
Pernod Ricard (Paris)		€13 billion	Jacob's Creek, Bodegas Etchart, Mumm, Mumm Cuvée Napa, Perrier Jouët, Montana (NZ), nine Spanish wineries	Stolichnaya, Seagram's, Beefeater, The Glenlivet, Chivas Regal, Wild Turkey, Jameson, Ballantine's, . . . Kahlúa, Martell cognac, Ricard
Casella Family (Australia)	10	Privately held	Yellow Tail	—
Brown-Forman Wines (Louisville, KY)	6.4	$9 billion	Korbel, Jekel, Sonoma-Cutrer, Fetzer, Bolla	Jack Daniel's, Southern Comfort, Finlandia, Canadian Mist, Dansk, Hartmann luggage, Jim Beam, Sauza, Courvoisier, Canadian Club, Laphroaig, Maker's Mark
Beam Wine Estates (subsidiary of Fortune Brands; IL)	3.0		Clos du Bois, Geyser Peak, Wild Horse, Gary Farrell, Buena Vista Carneros, Atlas Peak, William Hill Estates, Haywood, Canyon Road, Jakes Fault, XYZin	
LVMH (Paris)		€35 billion (€12 billion in revenue)	Moet & Chandon, Veuve Clicquot, Dom Pérignon, Riunart, Krug, Château d'Yquem, Cheval Blanc, Terrazas de los Andes, Chandon Argentina, Domaine Chandon California, Domaine Chandon Australia, Cape Mentelle, Cloudy Bay	Glenmorangie, Belvedere, Hennessey, Grand Marnier; fashion (Louis Vuitton, Givenchy, etc.); perfume (Dior); watches (TAG Heuer, etc.)

SOURCE: Case sales data are from *Wine Business Monthly* Top 30 U.S. companies. Some brand data collected from corporate websites.

The longer fermentation time of natural yeasts is generally associated with wines that have more character on the palate, as fewer aromatic compounds are lost during fermentation. The difficulty, from a winemaker's perspective, is that the natural yeasts may not be present in large enough quantities. If the yeasts are too slow to start fermentation, unwanted bacteria may multiply and spoil the product. A winemaker can tilt the balance back in favor of the wild yeasts by adding sulfur dioxide to the crushed grapes and keeping the fermentation temperatures cool.

But the risk is still too high for many winemakers, who prefer to kill the wild yeasts with sulfur compounds and introduce cultured strains. Cultured yeasts are more stable and produce faster fermentations. Some strains of yeast have been modified to combat some of the microbiological challenges in winemaking. Indeed, the first genetically modified (GM) yeast strain for wine, ML01, is now commercially available in the United States. If the use of GM yeasts became widespread or well known, however, there could be consumer backlash in some countries, and it would not currently be permitted within the EU.[13]

Although buying enzymes and cultured yeasts runs up the bill for winemakers, it reduces the risks of spoilage and increases the stability of the end product. Tweaks along the way can lead to a tailor-made product that can be tested on focus groups. And making wine using cultured yeasts and added enzymes accords well with the corporate view of wine, which seeks to ensure consistency and increase appeal to consumers.

→>-<-

Another issue that determines the types of wines available to retailers and consumers is the market power of large corporations with broad wine portfolios. As many distributors, such as Southern, bulk up through growth and acquisitions, the producers sat on their hands. In 2000, when Vivendi Universal made a bid to take over Seagram's for its media assets, the 250 wines and spirits brands owned by Seagram's, were up for sale. Consolidation in wine and spirits accelerated. Constellation started making acquisitions to rival Gallo, traditionally the biggest producer, and finally outstripped Gallo with its acquisition of Robert Mondavi in 2004. With the acquisition of Vincor in 2006, Constellation's worldwide production exceeded 100 million cases. Gallo remains a privately held company, with an estimated 75 million cases of wine sold in 2005 and $3 billion in revenue (not including related entities such as Gallo Glass).[14] Constellation, a publicly traded company, sells fewer cases in the United States than Gallo but derives more revenue from those sales: $4.6 billion from all of its U.S. activity for 2005. Each of these companies controls about one-fifth of wine sales in the United States.

As spirits companies acquire wine properties, they may wield more power over distributors and retailers. Brown-Forman, Beam Wine Group, Pernod, LVMH, and, most significantly, Diageo all have large, highly sought-after spirits brands (see table 8). When Diageo acquired Seagram's wine and spirits, they demanded that their distributors provide them with exclusive sales teams.[15] Would it be far-fetched to imagine that the company might expect its distributors to place a large order when a new product is announced? Might it make availability of desirable wine and spirits labels incontingent on purchases of a new product or a flagging one? Such "tied" sales are illegal in most states but legal in Europe, and often the purchase of one case of a château's top wine is tied to the purchase of, say, ten cases of a lesser wine from the château. Powerful companies like Diageo, which has a market capitalization of $48 billion, may be dictating terms to some distributors, arranging sales directly with big retail chains and setting the markups for distributors instead of being told what they will be.

This increasingly corporate atmosphere of the wine world irks Ira Smith, an independent retailer in rural Kent, Connecticut. He told me that as brands grow more important, "we have more and more people controlling this business who don't know, don't care, and can't even pronounce anything about wine." To him and many other enthusiasts, wine is more than simply another consumer commodity.

Regarding the possibility that the recent large retailers like Costco might purchase directly from wine producers, bypassing distributors and their markups, Smith urges caution. "I stock 5,300 SKUs, they stock 182," he said. "If you like one-dimensional, unsophisticated, dumbed down, monochromatic wines, that are made the same ways chemicals are, then you'll be very happy. If you like a weird wine with notes of shaved cocoa, or a Cahors, or a Malbec that doesn't taste like a Merlot, then you'll be out of luck."[16]

Consumers who have purchased a *cru* Bordeaux at a bargain price at Costco might dispute this point, but they are likely to live in Chicago, New York, or San Francisco. In competitive markets such as these, the range of wine available is second to none on the planet. Every winery in the world, it seems, wants to place its wines in the big urban American markets. Gone are the days of foreign producers keeping special wines for the home market and selling lesser wines to the United States. Not only is the American market forecast to outgrow all

others, but it also has a lot of prestige. America is home to many influential media outlets as well as trendsetters in fashion, entertainment,
and gastronomy. It is an honor for a wine producer anywhere to make
it on to the wine lists of the top restaurants in New York, Washington,
and other important U.S. cities. In more remote areas, however, especially where wine consumption rates are low, it is hard to find limited-
production wines; instead, consumers are likely to run into a wall of
mass-produced wines. The distributors play a key role in structuring
the market and determining which wines are available.

Jeff Lefevere, the Indianapolis wine enthusiast quoted in chapter 1,
describes his local situation:

> Unfortunately, we're locked up by big distributors, so as they move more
> and more towards category management and fewer SKUs, you just can't
> seem to find the gems . . . and the few wine shops we do have that have a
> crafted selection, they know who else in town is carrying some of the
> harder-to-find bottles, and I firmly believe that they charge premiums if
> they are the only local market store carrying something. I had a situation
> with a local wine shop that was charging $32 for a Rombauer Zinfandel
> that was *everywhere* on the Internet for at most $24. But, if you really
> want a bottle, you have no other choice but to grin and bear it. Stuff like
> that happens all the time. This is why going to New York City and going
> to the wine shops was like Shangri-la for me. I saw domestic wines that I
> would never see in Indiana.[17]

But it is also arguable that today, more consumers are getting the
wines they want from large producers. Whoever is buying the 8.6 million cases of Yellow Tail certainly isn't complaining. Four companies
control two-thirds of the volume and one-half of the value of wine
made in the United States. But even these big companies are proud of
the diversity of their brands. Jose Fernandez, who runs Constellation
Wines US, told *Wine Business Monthly:* "We're seeing a consolidation
of suppliers but not brands; there's probably more variety and frag-
mentation of wine styles and brands than there ever has been."[18]
Acquisitions are strategic and often fill holes in a corporate portfolio,
as with Diageo's acquisition of Chalone, which provided more Bur-
gundy-style reds to complement their heavily Bordeaux-style portfolio.

It's not impossible for corporations to make and sell good wine, and
even very good wine; after all, quality wine making is capital-intensive,
and these companies certainly have the capital. Those selling wine are
unanimous that the market is very competitive, and there is no room
for poor quality or weak marketing. A large wine producer can bur-
nish its image by using profits from the sales of bulk wine to build up

the reputation of its prestige wines.[19] When brands and wineries are traded, the acquiring company often pays a premium, so the management has a strong incentive not to let the new brands languish. Constellation has provided more autonomy to its prestige brands under its Icon Estates umbrella, which operates out of Napa rather than a corporate headquarters in Fairport, New York.

Yet some consumers still complain of a similarity in taste even among the most expensive wines. Even if lower-priced offerings are tailored to please the consumer, surely the most expensive and highly prized wines must reflect the unique qualities of the vineyard? Perhaps not, if they are made to the specifications of a winemaker who travels the world advising client producers.

-+->-<+-

Not much happens at the Gilberto Lavaque airstrip. The town it serves, Cafayate, lies about 1,000 miles northwest of Buenos Aires in the region of Salta, near Argentina's borders with Chile and Bolivia. At 28 degrees south of the equator and a mile above sea level, one might expect the area's main crop to be coffee. Instead, it is wine. The dusty airfield is named after a member of the Lavaque family, which has been making wine in the high valley of Cafayate since the 1870s, though the current generation resides in Buenos Aires. The airstrip eases their journey to this remote region. But the Lavaques are not the only ones to land a private plane at the airstrip: so does the winemaker Michel Rolland.

Perhaps nobody epitomizes the global nature of the contemporary wine trade more than Rolland. Although he and his wife own a winery in Bordeaux and vineyards in Argentina, his main work is as a consulting enologist to more than one hundred wineries on four continents. He has been coming to this remote corner of Argentina since 1987 to help Arnaldo Etchart make wines at San Pedro de Yacochuya. The Malbec received 95 points from Robert Parker for the 2000 vintage and sells for $65—when you can find it.

Rolland's imprimatur can spell success in the export markets. In the past, Argentine wines were hardly exported at all: produced in vast quantity, they were consumed in prodigious amounts domestically, and in the 1960s national per capita consumption rates outstripped those of France. But as the domestic wine market started to decline with the rise of beer and soda consumption, the winemakers were stuck with a glut. In the 1980s, hyperinflation added to their pain, and by the 1990s, they were seeking export markets and sales in hard currency.

Because the foreign markets were already weighed down with wines from other countries, the only way for Argentine wines to make a splash was through quality. The shift to better wines was driven partly by homegrown talent, such as Nicolas Catena, who owns Catena Zapata, and partly by overseas advisers, such as Rolland from France and Paul Hobbs from America.

Although his services are in great demand, Rolland's critics consider him to have a one-size-fits-all approach to winemaking. Indeed, in *Mondovino*, the art-house documentary about globalization in the wine world, Rolland and Robert Parker figure as something of an axis of evil. The film suggests that they collaborate to encourage the production of wines of a similar style—rich, fruity, intense, and extracted—all over the world. In the documentary, which was panned in the United States but praised in France, Rolland coaches winemakers to use more micro-oxygenation, a technique of running fine bubbles through the wine to smooth the tannins. Even if this was exaggerated, Rolland does impose a certain distinctive signature on his wines from around the world. And it is a signature that Robert Parker likes.

→>◄–

Wine consumers love critics. While moviegoers routinely ignore them—witness the success of summer blockbusters despite the usual critical thumbs-down—many wine consumers slavishly follow the lead of the top critics. Several factors contribute to this. The number of wines on the market vastly exceeds the number of Hollywood movies that come out each year, so consumers can feel swamped with choices. Also, buying wine can be complicated. Just when you've learned to recognize the producer and the place for New World wines, you move on to European wines and find there's no grape variety on the label—and what about the vintage? The critic can offer an independent guide to quality, more reliable than the producer's marketing materials. Finally, the "invisible hand" of the market cannot always set a price on quality—especially in areas of incomplete information. Joseph Stiglitz, the Nobel Prize–winning economist, has said that quality, with its power to flummox the market mechanism, is so powerful that it can lead to the "repeal" of the law of supply and demand, as buyers and sellers may have differing ideas of quality or different amounts of information.[20] As John Maynard Keynes noted in his *General Theory of Employment, Interest, and Money,* to try to predict the winner of a lineup of one hundred contestants in a beauty contest, the best tactic is to "favor an average definition of beauty rather than a personal one."[21] Reviews by a powerful critic can organize the wine market into good, better and best, and prices will follow suit. But they may also steer consumers away from wines they might otherwise prefer.

Although *Wine Spectator* magazine is influential, no single critic is more important than Robert Parker. He has said as much himself: "You can have the critic for the *New York Times* shut down a restaurant or a play, but he doesn't have any effect in Tokyo, or Singapore or Paris. Where the difference with me is, here in Monkton, Maryland, the impact is worldwide, not Baltimore or New York."[22] An attorney by training, Parker traces his breakthrough moment in the wine world to the time when he tasted samples of the 1982 Bordeaux vintage and declared it an extraordinary year, contradicting several British writers. His enduring loyalty to French wines is reciprocated: he was awarded France's highest civilian award, the Legion of Honor, by President Jacques Chirac.

Parker's tasting notes are evocative, and his enthusiasm is often infectious. Consider his note on Larkmead, from Calistoga, California:

> The 2002 cabernet sauvignon Estate (100% cabernet sauvignon, 3,500 cases produced) is performing even better from bottle than it did from cask. It is a sexy, supple cabernet offering a dense saturated purple color, and a big, full-bodied, heady bouquet of black fruits, melted licorice, and smoke. This fleshy, hedonistic cabernet sauvignon will have huge crowd appeal, and should fare well in blind tastings. Enjoy it over the next 10–15 years.[23]

He has also described a Zinfandel as "balls to the wall," likened a Margaux to "a towering skyscraper in the mouth," and written of one Châteauneuf-du-Pape as "pure sex in a bottle. . . . This will make even the most puritanical American rethink his antidrinking policy."[24]

Parker trumpets his independence from the industry, and his bimonthly newsletter accepts no advertising, unlike *Wine Spectator*, a glossy, large-format magazine with a higher circulation. Parker hails Ralph Nader as his inspiration, and he's perhaps at his best in his consumer-advocate mode, cutting through the producer's mumbo jumbo about appellations and history and being willing to slam a producer of a $100 bottle of wine with a middling score. He has developed a devout following: legions of followers subscribe to his newsletter and website and buy his various thick books. With a good review from Parker, the wines fly out the door, often before even touching down in the store (if they are sold as future arrivals). If a wine does not receive a blessing from Parker, it may need an additional push from another critic to move it off the store shelves. An old industry saw runs, "If it gets more than 90 points, you can't stock it; if it gets less than 90 points, you can't sell it."

Good wine reviews are so coveted that wineries may hire a consulting winemaker, like Michel Rolland, or go further and use a firm in Napa called Enologix, which virtually guarantees success. Enologix helps wineries, including some A-list wineries, tailor their wines so that they will receive high scores from Parker and James Laube, *Wine Spectator*'s California correspondent. Leo McCloskey, who founded Enologix fifteen years ago and has a PhD in chemical ecology, bypasses the more traditional wine characteristics of sugar, alcohol, and acidity and focuses instead on more obscure chemical elements that occur naturally, such as terpenes, phenols, and anthocyanins. Phenols have been receiving increased attention from other winemakers, but anthocyanins remain an Enologix specialty. According to an extended profile in the *New York Times*, McCloskey advises his clients on ways to manipulate these background components to arrive at a jammy red wine with soft tannins that will score better.[25] He claims to be able to predict a wine's final score within two and a half points. He expects his clients to become self-sufficient in their chemical analyses, telling the *Times* that ultimately, "I'll be replaced by customer-management software." Although Julio Gallo's era of the "magic chef" winemaker seems laughably outdated, lots of wine is still made in the lab. But these days, the raw material is of higher quality and the procedures more refined than Gallo's in the 1950s, and the final product certainly fetches a higher price than the Gallo brothers could ever have imagined.

→>-<-

There are two criticisms of Parker: the style of wines he likes and his scores. Parker arranges blind tastings with a hundred wines in a morning in his office, swirling, sniffing, spitting, and scribbling to arrive at a score for each. Such a format, critics suggest, favors big, concentrated wines that can shout louder than the rest. These high-octane fruit bombs might do well under the fluorescent lights of the tasting room but seem overpowering by candlelight, consumed with a meal. As David Darlington has written, "For the same reason that a thundering symphony or screaming guitar solo may not make the best dinner music, wines that do poorly in competitive tastings sometimes fare better with meals than those attention-grabbing ones that impress judges in isolation."[26] And if the likes of consulting winemakers such as Rolland or Helen Turley or the chemists at Enologix prevail, this style of wine will crowd out others and perhaps eclipse the nuances of *terroir.*

Despite Parker's knack for writing vivid and alluring tasting notes, he is known best by consumers and stores for his numerical scores, which are assigned on a 100-point scale. While most consumers find this system intuitive, and many other publications have since adopted a similar scale, others bristle at its reductionist simplicity. And are the scores relative, within vintage and region, or are they absolute? And with Parker reviewing more than five thousand wines each year in print, how can one person have that many discrete taste experiences?

Many consumers find Parker's scores a useful guide for navigating the wine world and have no quarrel with it. Many retailers, too, love the simplicity of scores and plaster their shelves with flaps of paper boasting scores from Parker, *Wine Spectator,* or another critic.

But that's just the problem. "The Rating Game has bred laziness, complacency and neglect on the part of wine traders," according to W. R. Tish, an outspoken critic of numerical ratings. "In turn, consumers have come to take for granted the premise that wines are 'measurable' and, moreover, that critics' opinions, seemingly objectified via numbers, are more valid than all other opinions, perhaps even their own."[27] If Parker really has a discrete memory of every wine he has ever tasted, as he claims, and can be certain which score a wine deserves, Tish continues, then why will Parker not undertake a public blind tasting to prove that he will always give the same wine the same score? Although scores appear precise, objective, and unchanging, they are still only opinion.

A wine-shop owner told me that her problem with numerical ratings was that "even if they tell you that a wine is good, they don't tell you if it will go with your chicken salad at lunch." Numbers make no provision for food pairings. They also assume that all wines taste the same all the time, which anyone who has tried an extracted, high-alcohol red wine outdoors on a summer day, or a fine rosé in the middle of winter, knows is a questionable assumption. The extracted style itself, lavishly praised by Parker, is not universally loved by wine writers.

Furthermore, the range of scores awarded has become truncated. On the cover of *Wine Advocate,* the scale runs from 50 to 100. But scores in the high 90s are not as rare as they used to be, and Parker no longer runs reviews of wines scoring less than 85 points. Has grade inflation crept in? No, Parker has responded; the wines are simply better. But *that* much better across the board? Ralph Nader became famous by telling consumers *not* to buy the Chevrolet Corvair. Robert Parker, by contrast, lavishes praise on the Rolls Royces of the wine world.

Another criticism of the point system is that wine consumers do not rate other qualitative aspects of their lives numerically. It would be hard to believe a diner who pushed back from the table and proclaimed it a 94-point meal—or the guest who rated your decor a 90, or the date who gave you a 72. So Dorothy Gaiter and John Brecher, the extremely popular wine writers for the *Wall Street Journal,* use a hierarchical scale that runs from "Yeck" to "Delicious!" Describing a wine with adjectives rather than numbers comes more naturally to most tasters. I would be willing to bet that a lot more consumers have described a wine as very good, rather than taking a sip and saying, "That's an 88."

Despite his current sway, Parker may be on the brink of decline. Richard Nixon declared, "We're all Keynesians now" when no other macroeconomic alternative appeared to work. Within a few years, however, Keynesianism was dead. Similarly, when ads for the Atkins diet appeared everywhere and Atkins shares started publicly trading, it was time to sell them short.

On August 23, 2006, Robert Parker's succession plans collapsed. That was when his heir apparent, Pierre-Antoine Rovani, announced to cheers and jeers on the Robert Parker Internet bulletin board that he was leaving. Rovani had been in line to assume a leadership role as Parker, age sixty, was cutting back. Parker stared into the abyss of his own obsolescence. To his credit, he reshuffled his hand quickly. Again using his bulletin board to communicate staffing changes, he observed, "The times they are a-changin'," and announced the formation of a new "Team America."[28] He announced that he had expanded the *Wine Advocate* to include five writers, including two in their thirties. Their assignments would be structured on regional lines, and Parker's own role shrank to writing about Bordeaux, the Rhône, and California. This restructuring has given his "team" more youth and breadth, but that very diversity could call into question the perceived objectivity and consistency of the *Advocate* score. Time will tell whether the new hires can avoid this pitfall. In the meantime, the number of specialized wine writers is increasing, ranging from Allen Meadows, who specializes in Burgundy at Burghound.com, to Gregory Walter of the *Pinot Report,* and they are waiting to provide advice to consumers who may tire of the *Wine Advocate* in its new form.

As the critics' territory is fragmenting, wine and wine criticism are being democratized. Consumers are now taking off the training wheels and trusting their own palates. Evidence for this trend appears all over the Internet, from vibrant bulletin boards to wine blogs (full disclosure: I have one) and online video clips to burgeoning "social networking" sites where readers can post tasting notes and keep an inventory of their cellars. Granted, when it comes to recommendations for trophy wines to cellar for investment or to drink on special occasions, Parker's opinion still reigns supreme. But on the question of which wine to have with dinner, Parker's influence has decidedly diminished. Indeed, like the appellation producers, Parker may be a victim of his own success. The wine consumers he has educated and inspired are now finding they may no longer need him.

Perhaps the most compelling evidence of this independence is a new generation of wine store owners who are ripping up the preprinted shelf-talkers and writing their own. Best Cellars, which has stores in several states, arranges its selections by wine style, from "fresh" to "luscious" to "big." Crush Wine and Spirits, which opened in midtown Manhattan in 2005, has staff-written shelf tags that talk about the wine in terms of its body, complexity, and tasting notes—and has a take-out menu flyer with wines arranged according to food pairings. Crush and other stores stock wines from importers such as Joe Dressner, who has made a career out of importing a selection of wines that is explicitly anti-Parker. Andrew Fisher, who owns Astor Wine and Spirits in Manhattan, told me that the store displays no Parker or *Spectator* scores on the shelves because "we're the ones who know about the wines. Our relationship with our customers is to be a partner in our credibility."

CHAPTER 6

Greens, Gripes, and Grapes

Soscol Ridge may not be a vineyard that many fans of Napa Cabernet Sauvignon know by name. But some of the grapes from this young vineyard, on a cool slope in south Napa, are destined for greatness: they are blended into Joseph Phelps's Insignia. The wine is a perennial favorite of collectors and critics and fetches $125 in a store—when it's available. After Phelps bought the Soscol Ridge property in 1999 and the company wanted to expand the vineyard's plantings, it encountered an unexpected set of obstacles: not rocky soil or the slope on part of the property, but fish, frogs, flowers, and Native American artifacts.

Just a year after Phelps acquired the Soscol Ridge property, environmentalists successfully sued the county for failure to enforce the California Environmental Quality Act (CEQA) in vineyard development. The suit was a first because the law had previously been used to stop only bigger projects, such as highway construction. As a result of the lawsuit, the threshold for environmental barriers to new vineyard developments was lowered dramatically: members of the public could now register an objection that could compel a lengthy and expensive environmental review. In this atmosphere, Tom Shelton, the chief executive of Joseph Phelps Vineyards, called in an engineer to devise a plan for drainage on the lower part of the rolling Soscol Ridge vineyard that would protect a possible wetland area on the property and prevent soil erosion that could degrade the habitat of the steelhead trout in the Napa River, as other projects had already done. He had no legal obligation to take these measures, but the move was politically (and environmentally) prudent.

This undertaking, however, was just the beginning of a saga. Shelton next discovered that part of the land might have been the site of an ancient camp of the Pomo people. He arranged for Pomo representatives to inspect the area for spiritual significance. They found none. But just to be sure, Shelton invited some anthropologists for a site inspection. They could not rule out the site's importance, so Shelton decided not to plant there, either.

Then a state agency suggested that the property might be a habitat for the wildflower Burke's goldfield *(Lasthenia burkei)*, which has been on the federal endangered species list since 1991. The presence of the flower would have precluded planting vines, but it was difficult to ascertain because they bloom only once a year, in May. However, after a site inspection, state officials declared that the property was not a goldfields site. Shelton breathed a sigh of relief.

Local environmentalists—the same group that had brought the earlier suit against the county—then suggested that the creek at the bottom of the property might be a habitat for the endangered California red-legged frog *(Rana aurora draytonii)*. They had not seen any actual frogs, but then again, the frogs are nocturnal. So Shelton invited biologists to camp out on the property for observations. After two nights, they found no sign of frogs.

The Soscol Ridge vineyard planting eventually proceeded, and now 72 acres of the 160 are planted to Cabernet Sauvignon. Shelton is still waiting for final approval on 30 more acres. He reckons that increased environmental regulations add $5,000 per acre to the cost of developing a new vineyard, as well as the opportunity costs of leaving the land unplanted during what can be a lengthy review period. That sum is not a huge proportion of the overall cost of a vineyard, but it is another cost of making wine in California and one that premium vineyard owners must now figure into new vineyard developments.

On a list of hazards to the environment, vineyards would probably figure near the bottom. But, as we shall see, a volatile mix of Baptists, greens, and greenbacks created a flashpoint in California winemaking in the late 1990s. The conflict contributed to a change in styles of grape growing and winemaking that now adds a distinct tinge of green to the red and white wines. By contrast, French vineyard owners have faced little resistance to vineyards on environmental grounds; indeed, they have used environmentalist claims to support their vineyards against urban sprawl and criticisms of the perceived homogeneity of wine made with technology.

While globalization presents a set of large-scale challenges for wine producers, wine production is fundamentally local. The micropolitics of land use and the environment frequently pose greater challenges in the day-to-day affairs of wineries than the vagaries of the global wine trade. Similarly, countering the trend of a rise of branded wines made for and tested on the consumer and sold around the world, many vintners are rediscovering the vineyard and using natural methods to express the *terroir.*

STALLING SPRAWL

In the late 1960s, prunes and pigs outnumbered vines in the Napa Valley. The dusty valley was thinly populated and had a diverse agricultural base. Wine grapes accounted for about a third of the county's agricultural activity. Grapes grew alongside walnut, plum, and apple groves, fields of hay, wheat, and corn, houses of poultry, and herds of livestock. In 1966 grapes covered 11,700 acres in Napa County, and the value of the grape harvest was $7,000,000.[1] Having seen how Santa Clara County, south of San Francisco Bay, had rapidly lost its agricultural and viticultural areas to housing tracts and shopping centers, a group of Napa residents, including key members of the wine community, succeeded in 1968 in passing an "agricultural preserve" measure in the county. One of several greenbelt laws protecting open space all around the Bay Area, this measure, then the strictest in the entire United States, sought to limit real estate development by establishing a minimum size of 20 acres for residential property. When the state threatened to construct a six-lane highway through the middle of the valley, conservationists and vineyard owners rallied the Napa County Board of Supervisors to lobby the state to relocate the highway, which it did. Some even proposed making Napa a "national vineyard," akin to the national parks, although the idea never came to fruition.[2]

As a result of these "slow growth" measures, Napa County had a rate of population growth far lower than that of neighboring counties over the following decades. Although no longer the one-stoplight valley it once was, Napa County had a population of only 128,000 inhabitants in 2000, while the population of the greater Bay Area had swelled to several million. Meanwhile, grape cultivation had tripled to cover 37,000 acres; it accounted for 97 percent of agricultural activity, with a harvest value of $221,000,000.[3] But despite its almost unprecedented success in curbing sprawl and promoting agriculture and a thriving tourist industry, the wine industry found itself under attack. It became a victim of its own success.

→>-<-

James Conaway called Napa "an American Eden."[4] With warm winters and cool summers, a rugged and dynamic terrain, its open spaces, low population, and proximity to San Francisco, it might indeed be considered a paradise. Along with the increased investment triggered by the 1971 Bank of America report, the international achievements of the winemakers and the rising prices of the protected land drew tourists eager to sample the luxurious but laid-back lifestyle of the wineries. In 1970 Napa Valley had a total of 180 hotel rooms.[5] As visitors grew more numerous, the larger wineries started to build tasting rooms, often big enough to accommodate busloads, and paved their parking lots. Selling wines directly from the winery was a boon for the producers because the wines were mostly sold at full retail price, but without any cut going to the middlemen. Furthermore, a pleasant experience at the winery could buy many years of consumer loyalty from visitors. Now additional marketing endeavors, such as dinners, fairs, and entertainment of various kinds are commonplace.

The growth of entertainment and tourism (which at one point even included a proposal for wine tours by elephant) threatened to displace winegrowing in Napa.[6] Some winery owners argued that increased development threatened to strangle the wine industry that had inspired the tourism in the first place. That prospect, combined with the creep of residential developments, led the wine community to propose even more restrictive measures on land use. In 1979 the Napa County Board of Supervisors raised the minimum acreage for property from 20 to 40 acres in the 30,000 acres of the valley floor, which was declared an agricultural resource, and from 40 to 160 acres in the rest of the county, which was protected as an agricultural watershed. In 1980, voters passed Measure A, which limited the growth of housing in the county to 1 percent per year. And in 1990, voters passed Measure J, which subjected any change in the zoning of agricultural land to voter approval. Thus any development project that would take land away from agriculture had to be put to a countywide popular vote.

The tourists kept coming. By the late 1990s, the wine country was California's second biggest tourist attraction, after Disneyland. Around

4.7 million tourists visit Napa County every year. As more than 1.7 million of those spend the night, the number of hotel rooms has risen to 3,012. Although other activities also arose, they were largely complementary to wine tourism, such as fine dining, visiting Copia, the American Center for Food, Wine and the Arts, or touring the increasing number of olive groves for olive-oil tastings. Many of these other activities are not land-intensive, such as balloon rides, or have some historic claim, such as the springs of Calistoga. Winery visits still rank as the most popular tourist attraction: going to Napa still means going to visit wineries.[7]

As James Conaway has richly chronicled, the politics of land use became even more highly charged as new, wealthy residents moved in, vineyards and houses crept up the hillsides, and the environmental movement splintered into two camps.[8] As prices rose for land, many professionals retreated to Napa and built large, showcase houses. Napa had become a celebrity playground where newly famous winery owners rubbed shoulders with big names from entertainment, banking, law, travel, retailing, and technology. Unlike the previous wave of urban escapees, who chose winemaking for hobby or profit, these new residents were often not directly involved in wine but were simply attracted by the region's gourmet living.

Friction soon developed between the newcomers and the wine community. The new residents complained about the traffic jams of tourists on Napa's main road, Route 29, about tractors blocking the roads, and about the noise of agricultural activity, such as the wind devices growers use to protect their fields from frost in the spring and fall. One industry old-timer observed, "It is very romantic—someone comes up here and says, 'Oh, I have a house right in the middle of the vineyard.' Then when you turn on the damned wind machine at one o'clock in the morning and he thinks he's on the landing ramp at San Francisco Airport, you find out whether he's a farmer or not."[9]

This friction led to a rise of the sentiment known as NIMBY, or "not in my backyard," directed at the wine industry. In Napa County and other Northern California winegrowing areas, a strange alliance took shape, consisting of new residents, social conservatives, and green activists united against the wine industry. These objectors made clear their preference for what had gone before—the pastures, range lands, and undisturbed hilltops—over the "alcohol farms" that had started to creep up the hillsides. Ironically, many of these objectors were newcomers who had been attracted to the area, directly or indirectly, by the growth of the vineyards.

A hard-line group of environmentalist campaigners won a number of battles. Their influence, combined with the shortage of land, led one vintner to tell me in late 2000 that "there is a de facto moratorium on new plantings in Napa Valley." In 1991, in the wake of Measure J, environmentalists, vintners, and other members of the community created a watershed task force to study sedimentation, erosion, and habitat conservation in the Napa River and San Pablo Bay. Its findings led to the implementation of a 1991 ordinance that placed greater restrictions on vineyard cultivation as the steepness of the hillside increased.[10] In 1998 the California EPA declared the Napa River "impaired" as a result of sedimentation, low water level, and agricultural effluent. These conditions threatened the steelhead trout *(Oncorhynchus mykiss)* living in the Napa River, as well as causing sediment to drift into San Pablo Bay. Other environmental problems included the loss of prominent trees, such as mature oaks, and the related loss of migratory birds, which found neither the shelter nor the insect life among the vines that they had once found in the forests.[11]

The success of Napa Valley wines, and that of the North Coast of California more generally, has led to the replacement of open fields and previously undeveloped forest with vineyards. These new vineyards have often been sited on hillsides that offer new soil with good drainage. As such, however, they are highly visible, which some anti-alcohol activists find offensive; and planting vines on steep slopes, removing existing ground cover, can cause soil erosion. Conaway describes David Abreu, a highly sought-after vineyard manager, and Delia Viader, a vintner, as "pilgrims seeking the flavor bombs of stressed, runty grapes" who "bled soil into streams into the Napa River."[12] But perhaps no winery owner irritated the environmentalists more than Jason Pahlmeyer, whose Chardonnay shot to popularity after it played a supporting role in the movie *Disclosure*. Pahlmeyer cleared trees to plant a hillside vineyard without a permit, only to realize that the environmental activist Chris Malan lived next door.

In September 1999, the Sierra Club's Napa Group filed a lawsuit against Napa County on the basis that the county had failed to enforce CEQA (California Environmental Quality Act) standards for farmland developments, and they named Pahlmeyer in the suit. This was the first time that CEQA had been applied to agriculture; its provisions had previously been limited to roads and public works projects. In early 2000, the county settled the lawsuit, and a new, cautious atmosphere for vineyard development prevailed. All plans to develop hillsides on slopes of 5 to 30 percent were now subject to CEQA and could require an environmental impact report, which environmentalists and winemakers agree is a lengthy and expensive process.

Emboldened by the legal victory, Chris Malan, then head of the political committee of the Napa branch of the Sierra Club, ran for a seat on the county board of supervisors. She had financial support from the ardent environmentalist Peter Mennen, postmaster of St. Helena and heir to his family's toiletries fortune.[13] The decision upset the mainstream conservationists, as they already had a representative on the board who was also facing reelection and was endorsed by the Sierra Club as well as the Napa Valley Farm Bureau and the Napa Valley Grape Growers' Association. "Everyone was calling, telling Chris not to run," recounts Conaway. In the election, Malan's 10 percent vote split the conservationists and threw the seat to the prodevelopment candidate endorsed by the chamber of commerce.

This flurry of environmental controversy caused almost all local wine organizations in California to focus on community relations and sustainability. The president of the Napa Valley Vintners' Association declared community relations his top priority. A winery owner from Sonoma described it as a "crucial issue . . . that consumes hours and hours per week." In other areas, such as Paso Robles and the Livermore Valley, environmental groups are active. In growing areas, such as Lodi, where environmental concerns have not come to the fore as they have in Napa because of a different set of players and economic circumstances, the trade group nonetheless reaches out to the local community as a key goal.[14] The statewide organizations of the Wine Institute and the California Association of Winegrape Growers have developed a voluntary program of sustainable agriculture practices for members.

SUSTAINABLE GRAPES

Doug Shafer had a problem with gophers on his vineyard in Carneros, between Napa and Sonoma, where he grows Chardonnay grapes. The gophers were tunneling under the vines and gnawing through the roots. Shafer put poison down their holes, but the gophers persisted. He thought about using a propane explosive down the holes, as he had done in the vineyards near the winery, but decided it was too dangerous. He figured there must be a better way to solve his problem.

One day, when he was reading an agricultural magazine, an idea struck him: why not use nature itself by introducing gopher predators

Figures 7a–b. A conventional vineyard (left) versus a biodynamic vineyard with cover crop.

to the area? Rather than court cougars, Shafer built nesting boxes for barn owls in the vineyard. A pair of barn owls and their young can eat a thousand gophers and mice a year. He also put up perch poles, which encouraged red-shouldered hawks and American kestrels. The new method of rodent control provided round-the-clock protection, as the hawks hunt by day, and the owls are nocturnal. The strategy was so effective that Shafer named the vineyard after the hawks, calling it Red Shoulder Ranch.

This sustainable approach to controlling problems in the vineyard appealed to Shafer, whose father had established the family winery in 1979. Doug had spent his early career using chemicals in the vineyard to reduce weeds. In those early days, his vineyards were pristine rows of vines with the bare earth beneath them. But this "clean" approach to vineyard management in fact was problematic. Winter rains washed away the topsoil of his most coveted Hillside Vineyard, whose Cabernet has scored 100 points from Robert Parker and can easily fetch $300 a bottle. Further, the soils had been depleted of essential minerals through intensive cultivation, as they had been vineyards since 1922. Fungicides, herbicides, and insecticides had been used in the vineyard, and chemical fertilizers had been used to fortify what was left.

Following the lead of John Williams at Frog's Leap, Shafer decided to take a more holistic approach. In 1989 he planted cover crops of oats, mustard, clover, and peas between the rows of vines. Growers had previously resisted cover crops, in part on the advice of herbicide salesmen and in part because they believed competing crops would reduce the size of the grapes. But small berries actually produce more intense fruit. Shafer found that the cover crops reduced his erosion problem, enriched the soil, and limited weed growth (see figure 7). They also provided a habitat for beneficial insects, such as ladybugs and spiders, which prey on insects that eat the vines. "It's not always about eradicating problems as much as it is controlling them," Shafer told me.

For help, Shafer turned to Amigo Bob. With a ponytail and a droopy mustache, and perpetually clad in sandals, shorts, and tie-dye shirts, "Amigo Bob" Cantisano may not look like a consultant to A-list wineries. But in the matters of sustainable agriculture, his services are highly sought after. He has been consulting on environmental strategy at Shafer for about fifteen years. Another of his clients in Napa Valley, the Honigs, had a problem with the blue-winged sharp-shooter, a leafhopper insect, attacking their vineyards, which produce a $75-a-bottle Cabernet Sauvignon. Amigo Bob suggested planting a bed of nitrogen-rich alfalfa at the end of the vineyard. With easy access to this feast, the sharpshooters had little reason to move on to the vines.

Despite the success of his environmentally friendly practices, Shafer has stopped short of adopting strictly organic methods. The organic approach eschews the use of most agricultural chemicals even in bad years, whereas those pursuing a sustainable approach reserve the right to spray. "We're sustainable to stay in business," Shafer said. "We employ 20 people. If it comes down to it, I'm going to spray to protect the business." This moderate approach is gaining popularity with wine-makers and vineyard managers around the world. In France, growers who adopt it call it *lutte raisonée,* or "reasoned struggle." They agree with the overall philosophy of organic farming, but ultimately they are pragmatists.

Part of the reason that purely organic farming is not more popular is that the certification process is arduous, sometimes to the point of being infeasible. Organic regulations typically require the use of ex-clusively organic techniques for three years before certification. That means, for example, that growers cannot spray chemical fungicides in the event of a rain at harvest. If they do, the three-year certification clock starts again. This price, in money and time, is too high for some growers and winemakers.

In the United States, the National Organic Program of the U.S. Department of Agriculture stipulates that to be called organic and bear the organic seal, a wine must be made entirely from organically grown grapes (see table 9). Moreover, it must contain no added sulfites. Some sulfites, which are antioxidants, occur naturally in winemaking, and sul-fites are added to virtually all wine to preserve its color and freshness.

TABLE 9. DECIPHERING ORGANIC

On the Label	What It Means
100% organic	Made from all organically grown ingredients. Cannot include added sulfites.
Organic	95 percent of ingredients must be organically grown. Cannot include added sulfites.
Made with organic grapes	70 percent of ingredients must be organically grown. Can contain added sulfites below 100 parts per million.
Some organic ingredients	Can be made from less than 70 percent organic ingredients, provided the percentages are stated on the label.

Because the USDA will not recognize organic certification from other countries if the wine contains added sulfites, it is extremely rare to see organically certified wines in the United States. The most common term consumers see is "made with organically grown grapes" on the label. This certifies that at least 70 percent of the grapes used are organically grown and sulfites are kept to a minimum.

Because of labeling and certification regulations, much of the effort to practice more sustainable winemaking may go unrecognized, and producers may resort to other means to advertise it—if they make the attempt at all. "The consumer wants it, almost demands it," Shafer said referring to greater environmental responsibility from wineries. One sommelier in New York City, Shafer recalled, sells cases of his Red Shoulder Ranch Chardonnay by telling the story of the hawks eating the gophers. In the era of Whole Foods supermarkets, hawks and friendly bugs sell. Messy vineyards are chic. But word of mouth is sometimes the only way to tell this story.

The push for environmental responsibility has had an additional local payoff for Napa winemakers: greater social peace. Their efforts have opened a dialogue with the environmentalists who had been attacking the industry. "We started talking," said Tyler York, head of the Sierra Club's political committee and a past president of the organization. "We just realized that [the wine community] put their pants on one leg at a time too." Chris Malan, the hard-line environmentalist, had a falling out with her financial backer, Peter Mennen. Mennen quit his job as postmaster of St. Helena after the U.S. Postal Service started to enforce a ban on pets in the workplace. (Mennen's electric green parrot perched on his shoulder at work. Seeking an exemption from the ban, he got a letter from his therapist saying that the bird helped reduce his anxiety. It did no good.) He is said to be spending less time in Napa after having acquired property farther north, in Humboldt County.[15] With new hillside vineyard development almost at a standstill, green the new orthodoxy, and regulations protecting any switch from agricultural to residential use of land, a fragile peace has replaced Conaway's "battle" over the vineyards of Napa. The sun shines brightly on the valley—and on Doug Shafer's solar panels, which he has just installed in order to achieve energy self-sufficiency.

→>-<-

On the banks of the Loire River in France lies the Savennières appellation, which produces white wines of supple power and finesse favored by connoisseurs around the world. Among the handful of producers in the region, one stands out—Nicolas Joly. Not only does he have an appellation within the Savennières all to himself—the Coulée de Serrant—but wines from his seventeen-acre vineyard earn high prices in the market and high praise from many critics, some hailing Joly's Coulée de Serrant wines as the Loire equivalent of Yquem and Montrachet. But Joly has also become the high priest of a movement of holistic vineyard management that is even more stringent than organic farming: biodynamics.

If the Shafer vineyards are untidy with their cover crops, the Joly property would drive a neat freak crazy. Along the driveway to the grand château, the rows among the sprawling vines are overgrown with cover crop. The soil is rocky, a blend of schist and volcanic rock. But the view is spectacular—the amphitheater-like vineyard looks over the trees to a bend in the Loire. A plow horse, fifteen cows, and a dozen sheep live on the edge of the vineyard, and Joly has diverse plantings besides vines (figure 8). "Modern farming is a huge lie," he told me.[16] The components of conventional viticulture—chemical fertilizers and herbicides in the fields, lab-manufactured yeasts and enzymes for winemaking—are expensive and make the farmer dangerously dependent on the suppliers. Spraying a chemical insecticide or fungicide may remove a vineyard pest once, but it often comes back and may develop a resistance to the spray, forcing the vineyard manager to resort to more expensive and harsher chemical treatments. Biodynamics takes a holistic approach to establishing a self-regulating ecosystem, with few or no external inputs and nothing going to waste. Gone is the monoculture of the vine—vines and bare dirt in sterile isolation—and in is biodiversity.

Figure 8. One of Nicolas Joly's fifteen cows at Coulée de Serrant. Courtesy Bertrand Celce.

To an extent, all forms of sustainable farming share this aim. But Joly adds something that Shafer does not: a shot of moonlight.

Every year at the autumnal equinox Joly fills a cow's horn with bull manure. He plants that horn in a place in the vineyard where he believes the astral influence is the strongest. At the spring equinox, he unearths the horn, dilutes the contents with collected rainwater, stirs it vigorously by hand for an hour, churning it vigorously in one direction to create a vortex and then quickly churning in the opposite direction to "dynamize" the solution. He then sprinkles minute quantities around the vineyard. This substance, known by the surprisingly sterile name of Preparation 500, is said to imbue the vineyard with vitality.[17]

This is not an elaborate ritual that Joly made up, but part of the biodynamic philosophy that dates to the 1920s and the writing of Rudolf Steiner. *Holistic* is an apt term to describe Steiner himself, whose worldview espoused practices for childhood education (still used in Steiner or Waldorf schools), architecture, and, just before he died in 1925, agriculture. In his last book, he outlined the practice of biodynamics, but the principles were not applied to wine until 1975, when

the Nikolaihof winery in Austria adopted the practice. Shortly there-
after, Nicolas Joly inherited his family property in the Loire. He tried
farming conventionally for two years but was frustrated by the frequent visits of chemical salespeople pressing him to buy their products
year in and year out. When he first read Steiner's *On Agriculture*, Joly
recounted to me, "I thought, here's a guy who died totally unknown,
and he didn't have anything to sell. Why not give it a try?" On first
learning about Nikolaihof's attempts, he saw them as "crazy." Nevertheless, he launched into biodynamics "with the faith of a coal miner."

Biodynamics can take several years to implement and may be more
expensive at the outset, primarily because of increased labor costs. The
initial interventions—weed-pulling, insect management, and leaf-
pulling—must be done by hand as the vineyard is weaned from chemicals. But once the ecosystem is effectively in balance, the costs actually
come down, according to many practitioners, while quality can go up.
For example, Joly told me that in the extreme heat wave of 2003, his
vines fared better than many of his neighbors'. As wooly and unscien-
tific as biodynamics may seem to outside observers, Joly's experience
has received support from the scientific literature. A paper published
in the *American Journal of Enology and Viticulture* studied adjacent
blocks of organic and biodynamic vines in California. The controlled
study found no differences in soil and vines between the two methods
for the first six years, but in the seventh (which coincidentally was
2003), the biodynamic vines had "ideal vine balance," with grapes
higher in natural sugars and total phenols.[18]

Biodynamics has attracted a growing number of A-list wineries from
around the world, and its practitioners often have the passion of activists.
From Zind-Humbrecht in Alsace to the Backus Vineyard at Joseph
Phelps, Pingus in the Ribera del Duero in Spain, Chapoutier in the Rhône
Valley, and Domaine Leroy in Burgundy, the list of wineries practicing
biodynamics often reads like a catalogue from a Sotheby's wine auction.

The harshest critics dismiss biodynamics as worth no more than the
manure used in dynamization. Others remain respectful of the approach
but dispute the causality, arguing that biodynamics itself does not
make good wines. Rather, they argue, wineries making great wines also
practice biodynamics, which imbues the practice with a golden hue.
Indeed, it could be seen as a "rich man's organic," given the prices of
the wines produced using the method.

Will biodynamics ever really catch on in Napa? Some think it is too
kooky. But the practice does have its American adherents, especially

among high-end winemakers. Others worry that it could give competitors an advantage. One Napa vintner told me that competition, more than cosmology, drove him to adopt biodynamics. "At our level, the competition is intense. We don't necessarily buy into the whole mindset, but we don't want to give our competition any edge," he said. And the list of American producers practicing biodynamics is growing fast: it now includes Joseph Phelps, Quintessa, and Robert Sinskey in Napa; Benziger in Sonoma; and Brick House, Bergstrom, and Maysara in Oregon, to name a few.

How do biodynamically produced wines taste in the glass? The practitioners point to the "life-energy" (biodynamism) of their wines. But it is impossible to control all the variables, such as vintage, producer, and vineyard, to isolate the effect of biodynamic practices. In 2004, a panel of wine experts blind-tasted pairs of similar biodynamic and conventional wines. In all but one of the comparisons, they preferred the biodynamic wine. Doug Frost, Master Sommelier and Master of Wine, observed, "The biodynamic movement seems like latent 60s acid-trip-inspired lunacy—until you taste the wines."[19] In their popular column in the *Wall Street Journal*, Dorothy Gaiter and John Brecher wrote their first column on organic (and some biodynamic) wines in May 2006. "Too many wines these days taste like they were made in a lab," they wrote. "These, generally, did not."[20]

Organic and biodynamic winemakers must decide whether to label their wines as such on the label. The agency Demeter will certify biodynamic practices in the vineyard for a fee (sometimes as high as 2 percent of revenues from the vineyard), and practitioners can then boast the certification on the label. But some winemakers doubt whether it is an additional selling point. Tony Coturri of the winery H. Coturri and Sons told the *Wall Street Journal*, "The general impression is that organic wine [means] less quality and 'hippie.' To me organic is part of the process, not the event."[21]

"The point of working organically is to make better wines," said Joe Dressner, a leading importer of wines from family producers, mostly in France.[22] "I think real wines have authentic aromatic and tasting character. The work in the vineyards and the use of natural methods in the winery means that the grape truly acts as an expression of a *terroir*. All this is to say I don't have producers who make organics or producers who make biodynamics. They make real wine."

-+>-<+-

Wine, "real" or not, lies at the heart of rural life in France. This fact may explain why environmentalists and wine producers have not clashed the way they have in Napa. In a country where vines have been planted since Roman times, it's hard for anybody to complain of an invasion by "alcohol farms." In fact, the converse is true: growers have to fight to preserve the vineyards.[23]

The idea of rural France, embodying small towns, ancient traditions, and rustic beauty, is important to citizens and tourists alike. The relatively late arrival of industrialization and urbanization in France has meant that citizens' ties to the land are still strong.[24] Many urban French residents seek a second home outside the city, not necessarily as a trophy of affluence but as a connection to their rural roots. Tourism, too, is connected to rural life in France, and it is big business, with 75 million foreign tourists per year visiting a nation of about 60 million. While many tourists come to savor the art, architecture, and museums of Paris, many also visit France's countryside to admire the landscapes, small-town life, and regional products. For more than a century Michelin has published guides to the small towns of France. Since 1903, riders in the Tour de France have pedaled around France, celebrating all its regional diversity on their 2,000-mile journey.

Wine and tourism are closely linked in France through a common emphasis on regional history and tradition.[25] Many towns and regions have wine festivals and wine museums. Wine routes have been a growth industry: tourists can wend their way along 270 different routes that point out wineries and other sites of historical and gastronomic interest. In the Loire Valley and Alsace, tours combine winery tastings with visits to historic castles. Some towns in the Languedoc tap barrels of wine in the town square for the annual Bastille Day celebrations. A senior wine official in Paris told me that producers take pride in their wine because "their [regional] identity is in it."[26] Other routes, such as the olive route in Provence and the cheese route in the Auvergne, highlight different specialty products. In Bordeaux, the *syndicat* that controls the appellations Bordeaux and Bordeaux Supérieur opened a tourist welcome center in 1999. But the bar was set at a new level when Philippe Raoux opened his $27 million facility, called "La Winery," in 2007. The Bordeaux Wine Council (CIVB) offers classes on wine in French, English, German, Chinese, and Japanese in downtown Bordeaux and plans to partner with other organizations to offer classes in London, New York, and California.[27] Bernard Magrez, the owner of several properties in Bordeaux, thinks efforts at education in the region are still lacking and opened his own education center in Bordeaux in 2006.

From a policy perspective, the most difficult objective is keeping the countryside economically and socially vital. Rural depopulation, policy makers fear, could bring a withering of the social life that is so important to both tourism and the national image. Viticulture is also seen as environmentally beneficial. Thus not only are wines and vines considered a part of the national identity and heritage that merits government support, but they receive support from the European Union as well. An EU reform document stated: "All over the world wine is associated with Europe.... Vineyards are not just an attractive part of the landscape but also play an important environmental role, protecting the soil against erosion and counter-balancing depopulation in areas that are often not suited to any other type of production and offer no other employment alternative."[28]

Ironically, the place where rural and viticultural identity is threatened most is in and around the most cherished and pricey vineyards of Bordeaux, particularly the left bank. As in California, some winegrowing areas that lie close to cities, often some of the best growing areas, have come under pressure from urban and suburban sprawl. The most glaring example is the Île-de-France region around Paris, where the only reminder of the once-abundant vineyards is a small set of vines on a hillside in the 20th arrondissement.[29] In Bordeaux, preserving the *terroir*—including a first growth that the city almost swallowed—has been more successful.

Graves lies on the outskirts of the city of Bordeaux. Or it did. During the 1960s, most land-use planning was still under the control of the central state and city mayors. The mayor of Bordeaux, Jacques Chaban-Delmas, who had ambitions to enter national politics, favored industry over vines, and his policies led to a period of sprawl. He sought to diversify the economic base of the region, which had been dependent on wine. Chaban-Delmas attracted the large aeronautic defense contractor Dassault Aviation, as well as other firms from technology and industry. In the resulting expansion of the urban area, thousands of acres of vines were lost to housing and roads. The hardest-hit vineyard was that of Graves, in particular Pessac-Léognan, lying just south of the city.

This growing area is home to several top estates from Bordeaux, including Château Haut-Brion (figure 9), the one château included in the classification of 1855 that was not in the Médoc. In the intervening decades, city growth has sharply reduced the size of the Pessac-Léognan winegrowing area. In 1875 the area under vine was 5,000 hectares. By 1975 that figure had fallen to 500, initially through phylloxera and then

Figure 9. Satellite image of Château Haut-Brion vineyards, surrounded by the city of Bordeaux. Courtesy Digital Globe.

through urbanization.[30] The city encircled the Haut-Brion property, which now resembles a private urban vineyard. The vineyard area of the northern Graves declined precipitously but has slowly begun to expand again. As a result of the formal recognition of the smaller Pessac-Léognan appellation (recounted in chapter 3), the producers were emboldened to protect the *terroir*. The vineyard area has expanded from 500 hectares in 1975 to 1,600 in 2005. Under the regional development plan, vineyards were given first priority.

The growers in Pessac-Léognan and elsewhere in France have several legal weapons at their disposal to protect their land. All are based on the sanctity of *terroir*, the view that the winegrowing area is unique and not replicable. St.-Émilion, the Bordeaux wine town, found an international weapon for local land preservation when UNESCO classified the vineyard as World Heritage Site. Under national regulations, according to the rural code, a *syndicat* can oppose development projects in the AOC zone that it believes would harm the *terroir* by requesting a review from the Ministry of Agriculture.[31] The ministry renders an opinion based on a study performed by INAO. Although its decision is not binding, the ministerial review almost always protects agriculture against sprawl.[32]

Since decentralization reforms in 1982, the regional and local government bodies have gained increased power over land-use decisions. This devolution has given winegrowers more influence over land use in their regions. Local government remains most important because this is the level at which land-use plans are developed. These plans attempt to balance agriculture with other uses, such as residential development, manufacturing, and retail areas. Most AOC vineyard land receives the classification "zone of natural richness," and no construction is permitted other than for agricultural purposes. When land receives this protection, then the owner can sell it only for agricultural use, not for commercial or residential development. The mayor holds the ultimate authority over the plan. In theory, plans should be designed for the long term, but in practice mayors and town councils often modify the plan more or less at will.[33] Thus the neither land-use plans nor the legal provisions provide an ironclad guarantee against urbanization, which is often more profitable than agriculture. In early 2006, regional planning authorities proposed a new highway bypass around the city of Bordeaux that would cross the vineyards of Margaux. In a burst of Internet savvy, producers set up a website and collected five thousand signatures against the proposal.

A leading American importer of wines from France and Spain told me that he looks longingly at vineyards perched on the hillsides outside of Banyuls, a French seaside town that is almost on the border of Spain. From the beach, where the Pyrenees slope down to the Mediterranean, the steep hillsides appear scored, as terraces run in horizontal bands to support the vines. Even though the importer loves the old vines of Grenache, he has not purchased any vineyards in the region; he says there is little summer labor, as the nearby resorts lure most of the area's workers. The steepness of the grade prohibits anything but manual work in the vineyards. Some vineyards have been neglected, as the sweet wine made from these grapes has also seen a lack of demand both domestically and internationally. So it is the resort owners in the area who are eyeing the agricultural hillsides. But they are unlikely to succeed in securing any prime spots because of the Société d'Aménagement Foncier et d'Établissement Rural (SAFER).

SAFER goes farther than most zoning regulations: it can prevent the sale and transfer of agricultural land for nonagricultural uses. It is a parapublic institution that can preempt sales arranged by two private parties. If the market price is too high, SAFER has the power to void the transaction, buy the land, and offer it for resale at a lower price, often to multiple bidders. SAFER can also prevent the transfer of agricultural land to a buyer who would seek to put in condos or a golf course. However, the organization does not always act in the interest of growers.

"This is socialism. It negates private property," Robert Drouhin told *Wine Spectator* magazine in 2001 shortly after SAFER had voided his agreement to purchase nine acres of vineyard in Burgundy on the grounds that he was paying too much.[34]

Perhaps that decision explains why Drouhin purchased his American vineyard land in Oregon and not in Napa. In Napa, his purchase could have triggered a negative declaration under CEQA and a public referendum on his plans, and forced him to produce an expensive environmental impact report. Although environmentalism has provided support for French vineyards, it has proved a challenge for the winemakers in America. In the premier growing regions of both countries, vineyard development and bureaucracy are likely to coexist, peaceably or otherwise, for the foreseeable future.

CHAPTER 7

Celebrating Diversity

On a rocky alluvial plain that the locals rejected as worthless for decades, several growers in New Zealand have taken an innovative approach to turning real property into intellectual property. Growers in this part of the Hawke's Bay region saw that their poor, rocky soil resembled the gravels of Bordeaux. The temperature, too, is similar to that of Bordeaux and the Rhône, as well as Coonawarra in Australia and Napa in California. Starting in the 1980s, and with more fervor in the 1990s and the current decade, the growers planted the grape varieties of Bordeaux and the Rhône, notably Merlot, Cabernet Sauvignon, and Syrah. In a country that made its name on Sauvignon Blanc, planting these red varieties was radical thinking.

The twenty-five wineries and eight grape growers involved wanted legal protection for this distinctiveness, but New Zealand has no law governing geographic indications. So the growers formed an association and registered the trademark Gimblett Gravels in 2001, complete with a logo. Together they own the trademark, which they license to any vineyard that falls within the two thousand acres they deem geologically distinctive. To them it is all about the *terroir* in the former bed of the Ngaruroro River. "No politics, no bullshit," said Steve Smith, a winemaker and partner at Craggy Range, whose first vintage was in 2001. "Either you're in or you're out."[1] This style of governance has more in common with an apartment co-op than it does with a French appellation.

The winemakers who put Gimblett Gravels on their wine labels are in contravention of no law, domestic or foreign, as it is not a place name, but rather a trademark. As a result of this protection and of the acclaim received by some of the wineries, Smith says that between 2001 and 2006 real estate prices quadrupled, rising much faster than those of the surrounding area.

This group of producers consciously called the Syrah grape by its French name, in part to distinguish themselves from their Australian neighbors, who call the grape Shiraz. John O'Connor, the owner of Matariki Wines, who first bought land in the region with his wife in 1981, also told me that "our style has more in common with the Rhône."

-+->-<+-

The growers in the Gimblett Gravels have blended a New World innovation with a respect for Old World *terroir*. One of the most exciting aspects of winemaking is the sharing of knowledge around the world.

In France, the cold winds of reform are blowing across the *terroir*. The European Union and the United States signed a preliminary accord in March 2006 to overcome twenty years of disagreement on place names and winemaking practices. Further, the reformist attitude of the EU agriculture commissioner, Mariann Fischer Boel, may pave the way for the adoption of New World style both in the bottle and on the label, particularly important for price-competitive wines. Oak chips and greater flexibility in varietal labeling will be allowed, for example. Her proposals to uproot huge swaths of vineyards and eliminate subsidies for "crisis" distillation will go a long way toward draining the surplus popularly known as the wine lake. It is sad to see generations of farmers displaced, and the reforms will no doubt be passionately opposed. But in the end, bad wine made with French savoir-faire is still just bad wine. Indeed, the low end of the wine market is a difficult place everywhere in the world: how much farther Australia's wine industry can rise remains to be seen, with a glut of grapes at home and consumer weariness of discounting schemes in the important British market (along with a growing consumer concern with "food miles" and increasing competition from Eastern Europe).

In France, the INAO voted in June 2006 to split appellations into two categories and allow more flexibility for those at the bottom to adapt some elements of the EU reforms. Some French wine companies have already adopted a more consumer-driven approach to winemaking and are producing fruit-forward wines with more descriptive labels, trends that are also being adopted for appellation wines. This is not to say that French wine is losing its diversity: there are still hundreds of styles, from Champagne to Châteauneuf-du-Pape. France's crown may have slipped, but it can be set right again.

French winemakers have never lacked the ability to sell wine at high prices, as the stratospheric pricing (and exceptional quality) of the top wines from Bordeaux 2005 shows. Any producer who can sell wines for $500 a bottle, or a company such as LVMH that can sell almost 600,000 cases of wine for an average of $44 a bottle, certainly has something to teach wine marketers in other parts of the world. But William Deutsch, who sold 7 million cases of Yellow Tail at $6 a bottle in 2005, also has lessons to teach the French. This global exchange of learning helps make winemakers more efficient as well as helping artisanal winemakers make their products more distinctive.

In America, domestic wine is growing more diverse. In 2005, new wineries opened at a rate of just under two a day. A growing number of remote regions are making interesting wines, and better-established regions are learning which vines go with the *terroir.* The Central Coast of California is brimming with excitement, as is the Santa Rita Hills region farther south. Beyond California, Oregon Pinot Noir is finding its groove, and in Washington State excellent wine is being made from the grape varieties of Bordeaux. On Long Island, Kip Bedell makes a standout Merlot. And Stone Hill Winery in Missouri does what King James's colonists could not: it makes a good wine from a native grape, the Norton.

But all this diversity from America and France—as well as elsewhere, with the rediscovery of indigenous grape varieties and *terroirs*—is dependent on consumers' actually being able to buy the wines at their local store. In a place like Indianapolis, the home of the wine enthusiast Jeff Lefevere and his wife, that means that a distributor has to be interested enough to carry quirky wines, such as a Merlot from Long Island or a Muscadet from the Loire. Distributors who do carry unusual wines may have an exclusive arrangement and charge a premium for them. Such pricing has little to do with supply and demand and a lot to do with politics. Robert Parker may be forecasting the end of the three-tier sales and distribution system by 2014, but the political clout and economic bulk of the largely anonymous players of the middle tier still make them serious forces in the wine market. Indeed, with respect to distribution, Europe is clearly the more liberal market.

There are signs, however, that entrepreneurs are finding new opportunities within the current chaotic legal structure in the United States.

Cameron Hughes Wines, for example, buys good wines on the bulk market and sells them directly to Costco in California, cutting the final price to the consumer. Several companies in California are taking advantage of a legal loophole that allows them to hold multiple licenses, spanning the three tiers, and they hold import as well as a wholesale licenses while selling wine to consumers directly over the Internet. Vinfolio is one such company, and its CEO, Steve Bachmann, told me that he aims to be in the lowest quartile (by retail price) of all retailers offering any wine because of these efficiencies. Another company, Crushpad, lets consumers buy a whole barrel of wine (the equivalent of 300 bottles), have a say in how the wine is made, and have it bottled with a custom label. It is then delivered directly to the consumer in one shipment. Michael Brill, the CEO of Crushpad, claims that bypassing distributors keeps the per-bottle price competitive. The next hurdle for wine consumers will be reforming the convoluted liquor laws of many states and gaining the freedom to purchase wines from the diverse retailers around the country.

As wine enters a bull market in America, there are signs of innovation and change in the existing institutions of distribution. That should make wine consumers all over America happy, providing greater access to the diverse range of wines produced around the world today. Discovering an enjoyable wine from another corner of the world may be exciting, but actually tasting it remains another challenge altogether—often a political one.

Notes

CHAPTER 1. WHAT IS WINE POLITICS?

1. Elin McCoy, *The Emperor of Wine: The Rise of Robert M. Parker Jr. and the Reign of American Taste* (New York: Ecco, 2005), 40; Hugh Johnson, *A Life Uncorked* (Berkeley: University of California Press, 2005), 40.

CHAPTER 2. SOIL AND SOCIETY

1. "La civilisation latine est . . . une civilisation de vignerons." Michel Lachiver, *Vins, vignes, et vignerons en région parisienne du XVIIe au XIXe siècle* (Paris: Fayard, 1988), 25; G. Durand, *La vigne et le vin* (Paris: Éditions Gallimard, 1992), 788. The French term *vigneron* is almost always translated as "winegrower." This is not an entirely satisfactory translation because wine is not grown; grapes are grown and then made into wine. However, I use it in the French context because it is common in the literature and recognizes that many producers grow their own grapes.

2. One hundred liters is equivalent to 133 standard 750 mL bottles.

3. Jean-François Gautier, *Les vins de France: Que sais-je?* (Paris: Presses Universitaires de France, 1994).

4. P.H.T. Unwin, *Wine and the Vine: An Historical Geography of Viticulture and the Wine Trade* (London: Routledge, 1991).

5. Jancis Robinson, ed., *The Oxford Companion to Wine* (Oxford: Oxford University Press, 1994), 787.

6. Henri Enjalabert, *Histoire de la vigne et du vin, l'avènement de la qualité* (Paris: Éditions Bordas, 1975), 139.

7. Marc-Henry LeMay, *Bordeaux et ses vins: Classés par ordre de mérite dans chaque commune* (Bordeaux: Éditions Feret, 1995).

8. Bourdieu makes a similar distinction in eating habits, noting that the working classes prefer the large quantities of *la bouffe* ("grub") whereas the elites prefer the refinement, delicacy, and cultural distancing of *la grande bouffe* (an extravagant meal). Pierre Bourdieu, *La distinction: Critique sociale du jugement* (Paris: Éditions de Minuit, 1979).

9. Véronique Nahoum-Grappe further argues that wine is a symbol of manliness, particularly among the working classes. Nahoum-Grappe, "France," in *International Handbook on Alcohol and Culture,* ed. D. B. Heath (Westport, CT: Greenwood Press, 1995).

10. Ibid.

11. For more on this history, see Philippe Roudie, *Vignobles et vignerons du bordelais* (Bordeaux: Presses Universitaires de Bordeaux, 1988).

12. Jancis Robinson, ed., *The Oxford Companion to Wine,* 2nd ed. (Oxford: Oxford University Press, 1999).

13. Eugen Weber, *Peasants into Frenchmen* (Stanford, CA: Stanford University Press, 1976). Even Barrington Moore noted that the French wine production did not lay the firm foundations for democracy, particularly compared to the political and economic consequences of sheep farming and the wool trade in Britain, which created a bourgeoisie powerful enough to rival the crown. "Wine growing in France did not produce the kind of changes among the peasantry, such as massive enclosures, that were the consequence of commercial agriculture in Britain." Further, the lack of sufficient capital for wine storage and the "legal privileges" (tariffs on wine from upriver) prevented the peasants from bringing their wine to Bordeaux for sale, instead forcing them to sell to the "chateaux." Thus, "in contrast to England, commercial influences as they penetrated the countryside did not undermine and destroy the feudal framework." Barrington Moore, *Social Origins of Dictatorship and Democracy: Lord and Peasant Making in the Modern World* (Boston: Beacon Press, 1966). Comments on wine and regimes, 46–55; quotes 48, 55.

14. Weber 1976.

15. The Midi, the region in the south of France that runs from the Pyrenees along the Mediterranean coast to the mouth of the Rhône, is also known as Languedoc. Cultural Languedoc and Roussillon are both in the Midi and today make up the administrative region known as Languedoc-Roussillon.

16. Robert C. Ulin's insightful ethnohistory discusses these issues as well as other important aspects of the "invention of tradition" and authenticity in the wines of southwestern France: *Vintages and Traditions: An Ethnohistory of Southwest French Wine Cooperatives* (Washington, DC: Smithsonian Institution, 1996).

17. Dewey Markham presents a thorough overview of the events surrounding the classification scheme in *1855: A History of the Bordeaux Classification* (New York: John Wiley & Sons, 1998). Also informative is book 4, chapter 1 in Charles Higounet, *Chateau Latour: The History of a Great Vineyard, 1331–1992,* translated by E. Penning-Rowsell (Kingston-upon-Thames: Seagrave Foulkes, 1993).

18. The Médoc and Graves are wine-growing regions within Bordeaux, on the southern banks of the Garonne. The Médoc, thanks largely to the 1855 classification, has enjoyed a reputation for producing the region's best wines.

19. Indeed, the hierarchy has proved more enduring than the ownership of the properties: whereas there has been only one change in the hierarchy (Mouton-Rothschild was promoted to first growth status in 1973, underscoring the classification's enduring importance 120 years later), only two of the properties remain under the same ownership as in 1855.

20. Robinson, 1994, 245.

21. Edmund Penning-Rowsell, *Wines of Bordeaux,* 5th ed. (San Francisco: Wine Appreciation Guild, 1985).

22. Stephen Brook, *Bordeaux: People, Power, and Politics* (London: Mitchell Beazley, 2001).

23. Weber 1976, 216.

24. As in Roman times, wine was often mixed with water as a sanitizing measure.

25. Powdery mildew, also known as oidium, reduced national wine production by 75 percent between the late 1840s and 1854. However, chemical treatments proved effective, and production was restored just as the rail boom began. Lachiver 1988.

26. Charles K. Warner, *The Winegrowers of France and the Government since 1875* (New York: Columbia University Press, 1960).

27. Ibid.

28. Robinson, 1994; Albert J. Winkler, *General Viticulture* (Berkeley: University of California Press, 1965), 725–28.

29. Unwin 1991, 285.

30. Christy Campbell traces the arrival of phylloxera in France to 21 rue Longue in Roquemaure, in the Gard. In 1863, a wine shop owner living at that address planted some rooted vines that he had received from a friend in New York. Investigators later traced the outbreak to this walled backyard vineyard. Campbell, *The Botanist and the Vintner: How Wine Was Saved for the World* (Chapel Hill, NC: Algonquin Books of Chapel Hill, 2005).

31. Warner 1960.

32. Warner states that the practice was limited both because it was illegal and because sugar was expensive. Ibid., 13.

33. Later they added "du Midi" to the official name after their successes led winegrowers in other regions to found similar organizations. Membership at one point reached seventy thousand.

34. By 1912, the CGV had thirty agents who investigated more than three thousand cases of fraud and secured six hundred convictions. Warner 1960, 45–48.

35. Gordon Wright, *Rural Revolution in France: The Peasantry in the Twentieth Century* (Stanford, CA: Stanford University Press, 1964), 27.

36. Details from Lachiver 1988 and Warner 1960.

37. Laurence McFalls, "In Vino Veritas: Professional Ideology and Politics in Viticultural Languedoc" (PhD diss., Harvard University, 1990), 3. McFalls provides a thorough analysis of the rise and fall of the "ideology

of viticultural unity" that sprang from the upheavals of 1907, and the relations between winegrowers in the region and the Socialist Party over eighty years. His focus on the Languedoc gives his study a focus on the politics of quantity and makes it a valuable complement to this study, which examines the politics of quality.

38. Other growing areas were also officially delimited within two years, including Cognac, Armagnac, Banyuls, and Clairette de Die. Bordeaux took slightly longer. Institut National des Appellations d'Origine, *L'appellation d'origine contrôlée: Vins et eaux de vie* (Paris: INAO, n.d.), 15–17.

39. Lachiver 1988; Unwin 1991.

40. INAO, *L'appellation d'origine contrôlée*, 19.

41. Because the Statut was aimed mainly at the high-volume producers of the Midi, I present only a broad outline here. Excellent, in-depth treatments are available in P. Bartoli and D. Boulet, "Dynamique et régulation de la sphère agro-alimentaire: L'example viticole" (doctoral thesis, Institut National de la Recherche Agronomique, 1989); Roger Dion, *Histoire de la vigne et du vin en France* (Paris: Flammarion, 1977); Lachiver 1988; and Warner 1960, chapter 7.

42. McFalls 1990, 120.

43. A common misperception in the secondary literature on wine, particularly English-language works, is that the CNAO (later renamed the INAO) was a large bureaucracy meant to control wine production. This was not the case. See chapter 3, which follows the more recent dynamics of the AOCs.

44. William F. Heintz, *Wine Country: A History of Napa Valley, The Early Years; 1838–1920* (Santa Barbara: Capra Press, 1990), 233–36.

45. Even today the U.S. Department of Agriculture maintains the National Peanut Research Laboratory.

46. Robinson 1994, 531.

47. Jefferson strongly disliked distilled spirits: "The ha[b]it of using ardent spirits by men in public office has often produced more injury to the public service, and more trouble to me than any other circumstance that has occurred in the internal concerns of the country during my administration. And were I to commence my administration again, with the knowledge which from experience I have acquired, the first question that I would ask with regard to every candidate for office should be 'is he addicted to the use of ardent spirits?'" Quoted in John Kobler, *Ardent Spirits: The Rise and Fall of Prohibition* (New York: Putnam, 1973), 32.

48. Cited in Paul Lukacs, *Vintage: The Rise of American Wine* (New York: Houghton Mifflin, 2000), 15.

49. In 1587, an English convoy under Sir Francis Drake dealt the Spanish armada a blow at the southern Spanish port of Cadiz. The subsequent plundering of the Spanish storehouses yielded 2,900 barrels of sack, a long-lasting and robust wine, well suited to sea voyages, that was a precursor of contemporary sherry. Sack became a favorite drink of the English: it receives glowing praise from Shakespeare's character Falstaff in *Henry IV, Part II* (ca. 1598). Lukacs 2000, 834.

50. Thomas Pinney, *A History of Wine in America from the Beginnings to Prohibition* (Berkeley: University of California Press, 1989), 13. Pinney notes that the French hold their wine production as an advantage over the English even in the form of chants and taunts such as this one:

> Bon Français, quand je bois mon verre
> Plein de ce vin couleur de feu
> Je songe, en remerciant Dieu
> Qu'ils n'en ont pas en Angleterre.

Clearly such an advantage would have been erased with successful English production in the colonies.

51. Ibid., 13.
52. Ibid., 17.
53. James E. Wilson, *Terroir: The Role of Geology, Climate, and Culture in the Making of French Wines* (Berkeley: University of California Press, 1998); Winkler 1965.
54. Pinney 1989, 24.
55. The study of railroads also offers some counterintuitive findings about the state and the market in France and the United States. See Frank Dobbin, *Forging Industrial Policy* (Cambridge: Cambridge University Press, 1994); Colleen Dunlavy, *Politics of Industry: Early Railroad Policy in the United States and Prussia* (Princeton, NJ: Princeton University Press, 1994).
56. Leon D. Adams, *Wines of America* (New York: McGraw-Hill, 1985), 20.
57. Lukacs 2000, chapter 2; Heintz 1990.
58. For more on Napa's rise, see Heintz 1990, chapter 5.
59. Lukacs 2000, 83.
60. John Hutchison, "Northern California from Haraszthy to the Beginnings of Prohibition," in *The University of California/Sotheby Book of California Wine*, ed. B. Thompson (Berkeley: University of California Press, 1984), 45–46.
61. In particular, Hilgard clashed with Charles Wetmore, a journalist who became a grower and the head of the Board of State Viticultural Commissioners. The local press played up the dispute. For more, see Lukacs, 2000, chapter 2, and Charles L. Sullivan, *A Companion to California Wine* (Berkeley: University of California Press, 1998), 346–47. The viticulture department was transferred to the Davis campus of the university in 1908.
62. Sullivan 1998, 51.
63. Pinney 1989, 356.
64. Mill called the Maine Law, and those that followed it, an example of "gross usurpations upon the liberty of private life." John Stuart Mill, *On Liberty* (Indianapolis, IN: Hackett Publishing, [1859] 1978), 86.
65. Pinney 1989, 432.
66. Gilman Ostrander, *The Prohibition Movement in California, 1848–1933* (Berkeley: University of California Press, 1957).
67. Although still low compared with France's 25 gallons, annual per capita wine consumption in America increased from 0.53 gallons in the preceding decade to 0.64 gallons during Prohibition. Ruth Teiser and Catherine

Harroun, "The Volstead Act, Rebirth and Boom," in *The University of California/Sotheby Book of California Wine*, edited by Doris Muscatine, Maynard A. Amerine, and Bob Thompson (Berkeley: University of California Press, 1984), 51.

68. Pinney 1989, 431.
69. Kobler 1973.
70. Louis "Bob" Trinchero, "California Zinfandels: A Success Story," transcript, *Wine Spectator* California Wine Oral History Series (UC Berkeley Regional Oral History Office, 1992), 3–12.
71. Quoted in Pinney 1989, 437.
72. Joseph R. Gusfield, *Symbolic Crusade: Status Politics and the American Temperance Movement* (Urbana: University of Illinois Press, 1963), 127.
73. Kobler 1973, 352–53.
74. Pinney 1989, 440.
75. Ibid., 441.

CHAPTER 3. AUTHENTICATING ORIGINS

1. Interview, Pascal Bobillier-Monnot, Centre National des Producteurs de Vin et Eaux-de-Vie de Vin de l'Appellation d'Origine Controllée (CNAOC), Paris, September 25, 2000.
2. William Echikson, *Noble Rot: A Bordeaux Wine Revolution* (New York: W. W. Norton, 2004), 25.
3. Ibid., 26.
4. Stephen Brook, *Bordeaux: People, Power, and Politics* (London: Mitchell Beazley, 2001), 195.
5. Pierre-Antoine Rovani, "The 1999 Red Burgundies, Part 1," *Wine Advocate* 135 (2001a): 43–61.
6. Yield is a difficult concept to translate. In France, it is expressed as volume of unfermented juice per unit of area (hectoliters per hectare, or hL/ha). In the United States, the yield is expressed as the mass of harvested fruit per unit of area (tons per acre). To confuse matters further, making different wines requires different amounts of fruit. To make 100 liters of wine (1 hL) requires 130 kg of red varietals or about 150 kg of white (160 kg for a sparkling wine). Using the average figure of 140 kg to produce 100 liters, one ton per acre is equivalent to about 17.5 hL/ha.
7. Jancis Robinson, ed., *The Oxford Companion to Wine* (Oxford: Oxford University Press, 1994), 1081.
8. Not all experts agree. Richard Smart, a consulting viticulturalist known as the "flying vine doctor," has suggested that low yields alone do not improve quality: there may be other variables at work, such as the vigor of the vines. He points to his own experience in the 1980s in New Zealand, where he experimented with different trellising systems and found "the higher the yield, the better the wine as assessed by wine judges." Richard Smart, "Higher Yields Cause Low Wine Quality," *Wine Business Monthly*, November 2005. Similar studies have taken place in Napa Valley, where wines from low-yielding vines were perceived to be more astringent. Dawn

M. Chapman, Mark A. Matthews, and Jean-Xavier Guinar, "Sensory Attributes of Cabernet Sauvignon Wines Made from Vines with Different Crop Yields," *American Journal of Enology and Viticulture* 54, no. 4 (2004): 325–34.

9. Brook 2001.

10. Data provided by INAO.

11. Brook 2001, 117.

12. Interview, J.-L. Roumage, past president, Syndicat Bordeaux et Bordeaux Supérieur, November 11, 2000.

13. Bertrand Duault, executive director, Association Française des Éleveurs, Embouteilleurs, Distributeurs, de Vin et Spiritueux, November 20, 2000.

14. Rovani 2001a, 44. Coincidentally, 1999 was an excellent vintage.

15. Pierre-Antoine Rovani, "The 1999 Red Burgundies, Part 2," *Wine Advocate* 136 (2001b): 10–24.

16. The châteaux came out ahead in the 1972 and 1997 vintages, when prices on release were lower than the futures sales.

17. Edmund Penning-Rowsell, *Wines of Bordeaux,* 5th ed. (San Francisco: Wine Appreciation Guild, 1985), 567.

18. Robert M. Parker, "For What It's Worth," *Wine Advocate* 136 (August 2001): 56.

19. Quoted in Brook 2001, 218. For a detailed discussion of the *place de Bordeaux* and how the wines of Bordeaux are sold, Brook is a useful reference.

20. Robert M. Parker, *Parker's Wine Buyer's Guide* (New York: Simon and Schuster, 1999), 128–29.

21. The headlines and quotation are from Philippe Roudie, *Vignobles et vignerons du Bordelais* (Bordeaux: Presses Universitaires de Bordeaux, 1988), 362.

22. Penning-Rowsell 1985, 148.

23. Roudie 1988.

24. Of several books recounting the scandal, the best is Nicholas Faith, *The Winemasters of Bordeaux* (New York: Harper & Row, 1978).

25. While the Gironde is the *département* in which Bordeaux is located, Aquitaine is the larger historical and administrative region of the southwest of France.

26. Quoted in Roudie 1988.

27. Penning-Rowsell 1985, 151.

28. Penning-Rowsell particularly stresses the role of foreign capital. Ibid., 148, 184.

29. Because agricultural producers are eligible for tax concessions, producers and *négociants* remain legally separate entities even when owned by the same group or family.

30. In 1963 there were more than 45,000 declared growers. CIVB, Service Économie et Études, *Marché Vin de Bordeaux,* 1999.

31. From Union des Maisons de Bordeaux, *Agenda 2000.*

32. Robert Parker, presentation at Vinexpo, Chicago, June 21, 2004.

33. Interview, Roland Feredj, June 6, 2006.

34. Oliver Styles, "Situation 'Uncontrollable' as Winemakers Go on the Rampage in Southern France." *Decanter,* accessed March 7, 2006. www.decanter.com/news/81357.html

35. Law no. 91–32 of 10 January 1991, relating to the "lutte contre le tabagisme et l'alcoolisme."

36. Charles Warner details the rise of antialcohol campaigns. Although government policy during World War I and the interwar period policies encouraged consumption, with soldiers at the front receiving a ration of wine and the founding of the Comité National de Propagande en Faveur du Vin after the war, the Vichy regime adopted a more restrictive policy. For drinks with an alcohol content of more than 18 percent (that is to say, not wine), the new policies raised the legal drinking age to twenty-one, prohibited advertising, and made bars display nonalcoholic beverages. Although these policies were scrapped after World War II, the government of Pierre Mendès-France (1954–55) adopted a two-pronged approach to the growing issue of excessive consumption: applying some general controls on consumption, such as prohibiting the purchase of wine on credit; and sponsoring a new series of research projects on the detrimental effects of alcoholism on the national economy. Charles K. Warner, *The Winegrowers of France and the Government since 1875* (New York: Columbia University Press, 1960), 200–206.

37. The French television authority even applied the provisions to international contests in which French teams were competing. This practice has enraged powerful professional sports entities, cigarette manufacturers, and beer producers, but the most vocal complaints have come from British advertising associations, who have complained to the European Commission that the ban on beer advertising is intended to protect the French wine industry. In late 2001 the commission initiated proceedings to bring the Évin law before the European Court of Justice (ECJ), claiming it created barriers to the internal market. On March 11, 2004, the Advocate General of the ECJ found the Évin law to be in accordance with EU rules, writing that "the French legislation under examination does not go beyond what is necessary to attain the objective of protecting public health that it pursues." The ECJ ruled the same way a few months later on the two cases *C-262/02 Commission v. France* and *C-429/02 Bacardi v. France.*

38. The first example is from the May 1998 Rapport Roques. The second is from the October 1998 Maestracci report, also known as the *Stage Report of the Interministerial Task Force on the Fight against Drugs and Drug Addiction*. The final two are recommendations of the Mignon report of January 1999. All are referenced in the *Union Girondine,* March 1999, 8–9.

39. "Let's talk about alcohol in high school, too," ran the motto of one campaign.

40. *Union Girondine,* May 1999, 9.

41. Philippe Feneuil, quoted in *Union Girondine,* March 1999, 9.

42. Jerome Agostini, Confédération Nationale des Interprofessions de Vin, Paris, November 20, 2000.

43. The last of four principles espoused by Entreprises et Prévention.

44. Between 1990 and 2004, French consumption fell 25 percent. In Italy the decline was 20 percent, in Spain 20 percent, and in Portugal 6 percent. German consumption rose during the period but remains lower than that of the southern European countries. *The U.S. Wine Market: Impact Databank, Review, and Forecast* (New York: M. Shanken Communications, 2005).

45. Interview with Jean-Luc Dairien, Onivins, Paris, September 18, 2000.

46. "The Globe in a Glass," *Economist* survey, December 16, 1999.

47. From Michel Lachiver, *Vins, vignes, et vignerons en région parisienne du XVIIe au XIXe siècle* (Paris: Fayard, 1988).

48. INAO data.

49. Onivins, *Rapport d'activité de la campagne 1998–99* (Paris: Onivins, 1999).

50. Penning-Rowsell 1985.

51. Michel Laroche, "Mayhem in the Midi," in *Peter Allan Sichel Memorial Lecture* (London: Wine and Spirits Education Trust, 2002).

52. M.T. Letablier and C. Delfosse, "Genèse d'une convention de qualité: Cas des appellations d'origine fromagères," in *La grande transformation de l'agriculture,* ed. G. Allaire and R. Boyer (Paris: Institut National de la Recherche Agronomique, 1995).

53. Interview, Louis-Régis Affre, Fédération d'Exportateurs du Vin et Spiritueux, November 20, 2000.

54. The five *côtes* are the Côtes de Castillon, Côtes de Bourg, Premières Côtes de Blaye, Côtes de Francs, and the Premières Côtes de Bordeaux, all on the right bank of the Gironde estuary.

55. Quoted in Charles Bremner, "Brave New World for French Wine," *The Times,* March 31, 2006.

CHAPTER 4. BAPTISTS AND BOOTLEGGERS

1. Kim Marcus, "When Winemakers Become Criminals," *Wine Spectator,* May 15, 1997.

2. Ruth Teiser and Catherine Harroun, "The Volstead Act: Rebirth and Boom," in *The University of California/Sotheby Book of California Wine,* ed. Doris Muscatine, Maynard A. Amerine, and Bob Thompson (Berkeley: University of California Press, 1984), 77.

3. Leon D. Adams, *Wines of America* (New York: McGraw-Hill, 1985), 233.

4. Ibid.

5. William Bonetti, "A Life of Winemaking at Wineries of Gallo, Schenley, Charles Krug, Chateau Souverain, and Sonoma-Cutrer," transcript, *Wine Spectator* California Wine Oral History Series (UC Berkeley Regional Oral History Office, 1997), 24.

6. Paul Lukacs, *Vintage: The Rise of American Wine* (New York: Houghton Mifflin, 2000), 115.

7. Confusingly, *table wines* means different things in France and the United States. In France, the term refers to the low-end wines, the *vins ordinaires,*

whereas in the United States the term refers to all wines that are neither dessert wines nor sparkling wines. I simply use the term *wine* in the American context, as the market is not stratified along quality lines.

8. Bank of America, *California Wine Outlook: An Economic Study of the Wine and Wine Grape Industries* (San Francisco, 1972). Rodney Strong, "Rodney Strong Vineyards: Creative Winemaking and Winery Management in Sonoma County," transcript, *Wine Spectator* California Wine Oral History Series (UC Berkeley Regional Oral History Office, 1994).

9. Strong 1994.

10. Adams 1985, 241.

11. On the thirtieth anniversary of the event, Taber expanded the story into a book: George Taber, *Judgment of Paris: California vs. France and the Historic 1976 Paris Tasting That Revolutionized Wine* (New York: Scribner, 2005), 199.

12. Ibid.

13. Although wines from California claimed the top spots in both the red and the white categories, one quantitative analysis has demonstrated that as a group, the French reds fared better than the American reds. Richard Quandt, "A Note on a Test for the Sum of Ranksums," *Journal of Wine Economics* 2, no. 1 (2007): 1–5.

14. Adams 1985, 239.

15. Quoted in George Taber, "Judgment of Paris," *Time,* June 7, 1976.

16. Some considered the American wines to not be as age-worthy. But in a highly publicized reenactment held in May 2006, tasters assembled in Napa and London tasted the same wines and again rated the American wines best.

17. William Andrew Beckstoffer, "Premium California Vineyardist Entrepreneur 1960s to 2000s," transcript, *Wine Spectator* California Wine Oral History Series (UC Berkeley Regional Oral History Office, 1999), 131.

18. The general idea was to improve quality by paying more for better grapes. Industry participants agree that Robert Mondavi and his winery played a key role in the introduction of the bottle-price formula. Its success is attested by the fact that the growers' organization and the winery vie for the credit for it. Robert Mondavi, "Creativity in the California Wine Industry" transcript, *Wine Spectator* California Wine Oral History Series (UC Berkeley Regional Oral History Office, 1985), 73; Beckstoffer 1999, 132–33.

19. Maynard Amerine, *Composition and Quality of Musts and Wines of California* (Berkeley: University of California Press, 1944); Albert J. Winkler, *General Viticulture* (Berkeley: University of California Press, 1965).

20. Material drawn from Beckstoffer 1999.

21. At this stage the areas were still known by their colloquial name *appellations.* Presumably to avoid confusion with the French nomenclature, this term has never received official sanction from the BATF/TTB. Instead, the grape-growing zones are called American Viticultural Areas, or AVAs (although, confusingly, the TTB uses the term *appellations* for growing areas before they attain AVA status).

22. Beckstoffer 1999.

23. Ibid., 137.

24. The largest AVA is the Ohio River Valley AVA, which spans four states and covers more than 16 million acres. The Texas Hill Country AVA comprises almost 10 million acres.

25. The state's crush (harvest) report did make further distinctions, however.

26. *Variety* and *varietal* are often confused. A particular type of grape is a variety; strictly, *varietal* is an adjective describing wines made from specific grape varieties, although it is frequently used as a noun.

27. Louis "Bob" Trinchero, "California Zinfandels, A Success Story," transcript, *Wine Spectator* California Wine Oral History Series (UC Berkeley Regional Oral History Office, 1992), 123.

28. Charles L. Sullivan, "A Viticultural Mystery Solved," *California Historical Society Quarterly* 57, no. 2 (1978): 114–19.

29. This material is drawn from Trinchero 1992 and Lukacs 2000.

30. Trinchero 1992, 65.

31. MADD ousted Lightner from its leadership in 1985 after she demanded a pay raise. Further, both the Better Business Bureaus and the National Charity Information Bureau cited MADD under her directorship for spending too much money on fund-raising and not enough on programming. Lightner reappeared on the national scene in 1994 as a lobbyist for the Alcohol Beverage Institute, lobbying against proposed lower blood alcohol limits in drunk-driving laws. "Founder of Anti-Drunk-Driving Group Now Lobbies for Breweries." *New York Times*, January 15, 1994, section 1, 7. The drinks industry, including some distillers, formed a group in 1991 called the Century Council to fight underage drinking. It is a sister organization of the French alcohol group Entreprises et Prévention.

32. The policy linkage was challenged, but the Supreme Court later upheld it in a 7–2 vote. In her dissent, Justice Sandra Day O'Connor wrote: "Establishment of a minimum drinking age of 21 is not sufficiently related to interstate highway construction to justify so conditioning funds appropriated for that purpose." "Justices Back Use of Aid to Get States to Raise Drinking Age," *New York Times*, June 24, 1987.

33. This tax increase effectively killed the wine cooler as a product. Coolers continued to exist, but their producers switched to a malt base as the source of alcohol because the tax was lower.

34. TTB officials revealed that they have a hard time keeping up with this law, as the number of small producers has increased. Although many of these are legitimate, some larger wineries have tried to take advantage of the lower rate by setting up new, smaller facilities.

35. Producers could not claim these health benefits on the label, which still carried the government warning. Not all producers complained, as they saw the warning as a protection from liability lawsuits akin to those brought against the tobacco industry.

36. Robert Parker, presentation at Vinexpo, Chicago, June 21, 2004.

37. Grgich also observed: "We do not macerate, and we do not go through malolactic fermentation in our white wines. We do not centrifuge, we do not filter grape juice. Our philosophy is to keep in the wine whatever comes from the grapes, like everything is in whole wheat bread. Our wines do have body,

and because of the body they have longevity. . . . I keep everything that comes from the grapes in my wines." Miljenko Grgich, "A Croatian-American Winemaker in the Napa Valley," transcript, *Wine Spectator* California Wine Oral History Series (UC Berkeley Regional Oral History Office, 1993), 32.

38. Beringer then belonged to Wine World, a division of Nestlé. Michael Moone, "Management and Marketing at Beringer Vineyards and Wine World, Inc.," transcript, *Wine Spectator* California Wine Oral History Series (UC Berkeley Regional Oral History Office, 1990), 70. Beringer, which has significant heft of its own thanks to sales of White Zinfandel, ultimately went to Fosters, and Napa Ridge was sold to Bronco Wine Company.

39. James Laube, Thomas Garrett, and Mary Ann Worobiec, "The Vineyard-Designation Trend," *Wine Spectator,* June 15, 1998.

40. Interview, Kent Rosenblum, March 1, 2007. Bill Sciambi, vice president of sales and marketing for Lauber Imports, provided the distributor perspective; interview, March 1, 2007.

41. Steve Heimoff, *A Wine Journey along the Russian River* (Berkeley: University of California Press, 2005), 181.

42. *The U.S. Wine Market: Impact Databank, Review, and Forecast* (New York: M. Shanken Communications, 1998).

43. See Warren Winiarski, "Creating Classic Wines in the Napa Valley," transcript, *Wine Spectator* California Wine Oral History Series (UC Berkeley Regional Oral History Office, 1994).

44. James Laube, "Napa's Name down the Drain?" *Wine Spectator,* May 15, 1999.

45. Interviews with Tom Shelton, October 25, 2000, and May 5, 2006.

46. Julia Flynn, "Grape Expectations: In Napa Valley, Winemaker's Brands Divide an Industry," *Wall Street Journal,* February 22, 2005.

47. Beckstoffer 1999.

48. Flynn 2005.

49. Carolyn Younger, "Continuing the Fight for the 'Unseen,'" *St. Helena Star,* June 8, 2006.

50. David Vogel, *Trading Up: Consumer and Environmental Regulation in a Global Economy* (Cambridge, MA: Harvard University Press, 1995); Bruce Yandle, "Bootleggers and Baptists," *Regulation* 7 (May–June 1983): 12–16.

51. Alix M. Freedman and John R. Emshwiller, "Vintage System: Big Liquor Wholesaler Finds Change Stalking Its Very Private World," *Wall Street Journal,* October 4, 1999.

52. When flying over Utah before the state repeal, some airlines prohibited the serving of alcohol.

53. Steve Boone, "Selling Wine in and to Large Specialty Stores: The Case of Beverages & More!" in Moulton and Lapsley 2001, 282. The TTB has prosecuted cases in which distributors have tried to buy better product placement with such gifts as CD players and VCRs.

54. Frank Sloan, Emily Stout, Kathryn Whetten-Goldstein, and Lan Liang, *Drinkers, Drivers, and Bartenders: Balancing Private Choices and Public Accountability* (Chicago: University of Chicago Press, 2000).

55. Lukacs 2000.

56. Details on the Arrowood winery are drawn from Richard Arrowood, "Sonoma County Winemaking: Chateau St. Jean and Arrowood Vineyards and Winery," transcript, *Wine Spectator* California Wine Oral History Series (UC Berkeley Regional Oral History Office, 1996).

57. Interview, John Williams, Frog's Leap Winery, October 25, 2000.

58. Daniel Duckhorn and Margaret Duckhorn, "Mostly Merlot: The History of Duckhorn Vineyards," transcript, *Wine Spectator* California Wine Oral History Series (UC Berkeley Regional Oral History Office, 1996).

59. Moone 1990.

60. Paul Franson, "Wine Marketing Companies Increase Roles in Industry," *Wine Business Monthly,* June 2005, 50.

61. Freedman and Emshwiller 1999.

62. Jordan Mackay, "Wine's High Stakes Boom Town," *Wine & Spirits,* April 2005, 52–61.

63. The distributors, also known as wholesalers, donate to whichever party is in power. " 'It's a good way to participate in the process,' said Peggy England, spokeswoman for the wine wholesalers association, part of the RNC's 'Team 100' group of $100,000-plus donors. 'It gives us the ability to meet with and to talk with individuals who are serving Congress and in the administration.' The group bought a table at the RNC dinner. It also contributes to Democrats, she said." Associated Press, 23 May 2001.

64. Jennifer Dixon, "Michigan Beer, Wine Distributors Keep Legislators under the Influence," *Detroit Free Press,* February 10, 2005.

65. Bill Bush, "Out-of-State Wine Prices Could Double," *Columbus Dispatch,* June 25, 2006.

66. Testimony by Tom Shelton, House Subcommittee on Livestock and Horticulture, *The Status and Prospects of American Wine Production,*106th Cong., 1st sess., 1999.

67. Ibid.

68. Clint Bolick, presentation at the Unified Wine Symposium, Sacramento, CA, January 23–25, 2001.

69. "Pataki OKs Direct Shipments into and out of State," *Rochester Democrat & Chronicle,* July 14, 2005.

CHAPTER 5. WHO CONTROLS YOUR PALATE?

1. Tyler Colman, "Partners in Wine," *Wine Business Monthly,* January 15, 2006, 103–5.

2. Interview, Bill Deutsch, September 7, 2005.

3. "Yellow Tail with John Casella," Grape Radio interview, October 31, 2005. www.graperadio.com

4. James Halliday, *A History of the Australian Wine Industry, 1949–1994* (Adelaide: Winetitles, 1994).

5. Frank J. Prial, "The Wallaby That Roared across the Wine Industry," *New York Times,* April 23, 2006.

6. Rob McMillan, *State of the Wine Industry, Forecast and Strategic Recommendations* (Napa, CA: Silicon Valley Bank, 2006).

7. "Two-Buck Chuck Creator Ups the Ante in Wine Feud," *San Francisco Chronicle*, May 18, 2006.
8. Testimony of Patrick Campbell, House Subcommittee on Information, Justice, Transportation, and Agriculture Committee on Government Operations, hearing on *The U.S. Wine Industry and Its Relationship with the U.S. Department of Agriculture*, 103rd Cong., 1st sess., August 24, 1993.
9. Daniel Duckhorn and Margaret Duckhorn, "Mostly Merlot: The History of Duckhorn Vineyards," transcript, *Wine Spectator* California Wine Oral History Series (UC Berkeley Regional Oral History Office, 1996), 120.
10. Data from Onivins.
11. Larry Chavis and Phillip Leslie, *Consumer Boycotts: The Impact of the Iraq War on French Wine Sales in the US* (Cambridge, MA: National Bureau of Economic Research, 2006). Chavis and Leslie analyzed data from supermarket sales, as tracked by Information Resources International. Two other economists found a remarkably similar financial impact using trade data: Jan Bentzen and Valdemar Smith, "The Military Action in Iraq 2003: Did the US Consumer Boycott of French Wines Have Any Economic Effects?" *Journal of Wine Economics* 2, no. 1 (2007).
12. Jamie Goode, *The Science of Wine* (Berkeley: University of California Press, 2005), 129.
13. On variations in policy support for and resistance to the introduction of genetically modified organisms in consumer products, see Grace Skogstad and Elizabeth Moore, "Regulating Genetic Engineering in the United States and the European Union: Policy Development and Policy Resilience," *Politics and Society* 23, no. 4 (2004): 32–56.
14. Wine Business Monthly, *Top 30 U.S. Wine Companies*, February 2006, and company data from Hoovers.com.
15. Wine Business Monthly, *Top 30*, 27.
16. Interview, Ira Smith, May 18, 2006.
17. Jeff Lefevere, personal communication, June 12, 2006.
18. Wine Business Monthly, *Top 30*, 16.
19. Michael Moone, "Management and Marketing at Beringer Vineyards and Wine World, Inc.," transcript, *Wine Spectator* California Wine Oral History Series (UC Berkeley Regional Oral History Office, 1990),
20. Joseph E. Stiglitz, "The Causes and Consequences of Dependence of Quality on Price," *Journal of Economic Literature* 25 (March 1987): 1–48.
21. John Maynard Keynes, *The General Theory of Employment, Interest, and Money* (New York: Harcourt, 1965), 158.
22. Abundant material exists on Parker, but one source stands out: Elin McCoy, *The Emperor of Wine: The Rise of Robert M. Parker Jr. and the Reign of American Taste* (New York: Ecco, 2005). See also Jonathan Nossiter's documentary *Mondovino* (Diaphana, 2005).
23. Robert Parker in *Wine Advocate*, February 2005.
24. Last quotation in Hugh Johnson, *A Life Uncorked* (Berkeley: University of California Press, 2005), 316.
25. David Darlington, "The Chemistry of a 90+ Point Wine," *New York Times Magazine*, August 17, 2005.

26. Ibid.
27. W. R. Tish, "Ten Reasons We All Lose When Numbers Dominate the Marketplace," *Wine Business Monthly*, December 15, 2004.
28. Bulletin board posts on Robert Parker Online website, http://dat .erobertparker.com/bboard/showthread/php?t=102310, accessed August 23, 2006; http://dat.erobertparker.com/bboard/showthread/php?t=103145, accessed September 1, 2006.

CHAPTER 6. GREENS, GRIPES, AND GRAPES

1. In 1970, beef accounted for slightly more of the agricultural output of Napa County than wine grapes. Poultry accounted for 60 percent of agricultural receipts. Napa County Agricultural Commissioner, Annual Report, 1970.
2. Leon D. Adams, *Wines of America* (New York: McGraw-Hill, 1985).
3. Napa County Agricultural Commissioner, annual report, 1999.
4. James Conaway, *Napa* (New York: Avon Books, 1990). The original subtitle was *The Story of an American Eden.*
5. William Andrew Beckstoffer, "Premium California Vineyardist Entrepreneur, 1960s to 2000s," transcript, *Wine Spectator* California Wine Oral History Series (UC Berkeley Regional Oral History Office, 1999).
6. Warren Winiarski, "Creating Classic Wines in the Napa Valley," transcript, *Wine Spectator* California Wine Oral History Series (UC Berkeley Regional Oral History Office, 1994).
7. One notable exception was President George Bush's unofficial overnight stay at the Meadowood resort on April 21, 2006. Bush, who swore off alcohol on the day of his fortieth birthday, did not raise a glass of Napa's finest but instead went mountain biking.
8. Conaway, 1990; James Conaway, "Bonfire of the Wineries," *Outside Magazine*, September 2000; James Conaway, *The Far Side of Eden: New Money, Old Land, and the Battle for Napa Valley* (New York: Houghton Mifflin, 2002).
9. Richard Maher, "California Winery Management and Marketing," transcript, *Wine Spectator* California Wine Oral History Series (UC Berkeley Regional Oral History Office, 1992), 67–68.
10. When the grade is less than 5 percent, restrictions are minimal. For grades between 6 and 15 percent, the restrictions increase, and a more detailed study of erosion control is needed. Obtaining permission for planting on slopes of greater than 15 percent grade is difficult and now necessitates detailed erosion studies from an engineer.
11. "The (Almost) Untouchables of California," *New York Times*, 28 August 2001.
12. Conaway 2002, 63.
13. Peter Mennen, whose family sold their household-products company to Colgate-Palmolive in 1994, is dedicated to the hard-line environmental position. He established the Mennen Environmental Trust with a donation of $15 million. Because of its not-for-profit status, the trust cannot lobby

directly, but it provides funding to the Sierra Club. Interview, Tom Shelton, October 25, 2000. See also Conaway 2000.

14. These examples are from the plenary session "Establishing Good Neighbor Relations," Unified Wine and Grape Symposium, Sacramento, CA, January 2001.

15. Interview, Tyler York, May 9, 2006.

16. Interview, Nicolas Joly, March 6, 2006.

17. Although *vignerons* have long taken into account the phases of the moon when bottling wine or harvesting grapes, the biodynamic philosophy carries this principle into consumption. Its most dedicated proponents claim that wines may taste best, for example, on "fruit" or "flower" days of the biodynamic calendar, as opposed to "leaf" or "root" days. In my observation, however, biodynamic producers are happy for consumers to try their wines any day. At a large tasting of biodynamic wines in New York City, I could only find out what day it was on the biodynamic calendar after asking a half a dozen winemakers. The one who eventually told me had to look it up.

18. Jennifer R. Reeve, L. Carpenter-Boggs, John P. Reganold, Alan L. York, Glenn McGourty, and Leo P. McCloskey, "Soil and Winegrape Quality in Biodynamically and Organically Managed Vineyards," *American Journal of Enology and Viticulture* 56, no. 4 (2005): 367–76.

19. Jean K. Reilly, "Moonshine, Part 2: A Blind Sampling of 20 Wines Shows That Biodynamics Works; But How?" *Fortune,* August 23, 2004.

20. Dorothy Gaiter and John Brecher, "Organic Wines Make a Natural Progression," *Wall Street Journal,* May 12, 2006.

21. Quoted in ibid.

22. Joe Dressner, personal communication, May 4, 2006.

23. Environmentalism in France is also weaker than in Scandinavia, Holland, and Germany. In the early days of the Green movement, France's Green party was not as prominent as those of some other European countries. Vincent Hoffman-Martinot, "Grüne and Verts: Two Faces of European Ecologism," *West European Politics* 14, no. 4 (1991): 70–95.

24. In the 1990s, one widely cited statistic was that one out of two French citizens had a grandparent who worked on a farm. According to employment figures from around 1950, nearly a quarter of all jobs in France were in agriculture.

25. This is a worldwide trend. See C. Michael Hall, Liz Sharples, Brock Cambourne, and Miki Macionis, eds., *Wine Tourism around the World: Development, Management, and Markets* (Oxford: Butterworth-Heinemann, 2000).

26. Interview, Jean-Luc Dairien, Onivins, September 18, 2000.

27. In 2005, the CIVB school had more than 2,500 students.

28. European Union Commission, *CAP Reform: The Wine Sector* (Luxembourg: Office for the Official Publications of the European Communities, 1999).

29. Urbanization has also claimed some quality vineyards around Paris. Michel Lachiver, *Vins, vignes, et vignerons en région parisienne du XVIIe au XIXe siècle* (Paris: Fayard, 1988).

30. Interview, André Lurton, November 10, 2000.
31. The legal basis for this process is Article L.641–11 of the rural code, specifically the law of July 2, 1990, on the appellations.
32. Interview, Jean-Louis Vivierre, CIVB, November 19, 2000.
33. Interview, Michel Dando, Fédération des Syndicats des Grands Vins de Bordeaux, November 14, 2000.
34. Per-Henrik Mansson, "Who Really Controls the Vineyards of France?" *Wine Spectator,* November 30, 2001.

CHAPTER 7. CELEBRATING DIVERSITY

1. Interview, Steve Smith, June 6, 2006.

Bibliography

Adams, Leon D. 1985. *Wines of America.* New York: McGraw Hill.

Amerine, Maynard. 1944. *Composition and Quality of Musts and Wines of California.* Berkeley: University of California Press.

Bank of America. 1972. *California Wine Outlook: An Economic Study of the Wine and Wine Grape Industries.* San Francisco.

Bartoli, P., and D. Boulet. 1989. "Dynamique et régulation de la sphère agro-alimentaire: L'example viticole." Doctorate, INRA, Paris.

Beckstoffer, William Andrew. 1999. "Premium California Vineyardist Entrepreneur, 1960s to 2000s." Transcript, *Wine Spectator* California Wine Oral History Series, UC Berkeley Regional Oral History Office.

Bentzen, Jan, and Valdemar Smith. 2007. "The Military Action in Iraq 2003: Did the US Consumer Boycott of French Wines have any Economic Effects?" *Journal of Wine Economics* 2, no 1, 75–83.

Bonetti, William. 1997. "A Life of Winemaking at Wineries of Gallo, Schenley, Charles Krug, Chateau Souverain, and Sonoma-Cutrer." Transcript, *Wine Spectator* California Wine Oral History Series, UC Berkeley Regional Oral History Office.

Boone, Steve. 2001. "Selling Wine in and to Large Specialty Stores: The Case of Beverages & More!" In *Successful Wine Marketing,* ed. K. Moulton and J. Lapsley. Gaithersburg, MD: Aspen Publishing.

Bourdieu, Pierre. 1979. *La Distinction: Critique sociale du jugement.* Paris: Éditions de Minuit.

Bremner, Charles. 2006. "Brave New World for French Wine." *The Times,* March 31.

Brook, Stephen. 2001. *Bordeaux: People, Power, and Politics.* London: Mitchell Beazley.

Bush, Bill. 2006. "Out-of-State Wine Prices Could Double." *Columbus Dispatch*, June 25.

Campbell, Christy. 2005. *The Botanist and the Vintner: How Wine Was Saved for the World*. Chapel Hill, NC: Algonquin Books of Chapel Hill.

Casella, John. 2005. "Yellow Tail with John Casella." Grape Radio interview, October 31, 2005. www.graperadio.com

Chapman, Dawn M., Mark A. Matthews, and Jean-Xavier Guinard. 2004. "Sensory Attributes of Cabernet Sauvignon Wines Made from Vines with Different Crop Yields." *American Journal of Enology and Viticulture* 54, no. 4: 325–34.

Chavis, Larry, and Phillip Leslie. 2006. *Consumer Boycotts: The Impact of the Iraq War on French Wine Sales in the US*. Cambridge, MA: National Bureau of Economic Research.

Colman, Tyler. 2006. "Partners in Wine." *Wine Business Monthly*, January, 103–5.

Conaway, James. 1990. *Napa*. New York: Avon Books.

———. 2000. "Bonfire of the Wineries." *Outside Magazine*, September.

———. 2002. *The Far Side of Eden: New Money, Old Land, and the Battle for Napa Valley*. New York: Houghton Mifflin.

Darlington, David. 2005. "The Chemistry of a 90+ Point Wine." *New York Times Magazine*, August 17.

Dion, Roger. 1977. *Histoire de la vigne et du vin en France*. Paris: Flammarion.

Dobbin, Frank. 1994. *Forging Industrial Policy*. Cambridge: Cambridge University Press.

Duckhorn, Daniel, and Margaret Duckhorn. 1996. "Mostly Merlot: The History of Duckhorn Vineyards." Transcript, *Wine Spectator* California Wine Oral History Series, UC Berkeley Regional Oral History Office.

Dunlavy, Colleen. 1994. *Politics of Industry: Early Railroad Policy in the United States and Prussia*. Princeton, NJ: Princeton University Press.

Durand, G. 1992. *La vigne et le vin*. Paris: Éditions Gallimard.

Echikson, William. 2004. *Noble Rot: A Bordeaux Wine Revolution*. New York: W. W. Norton.

Enjalabert, Henri. 1975. *Histoire de la vigne et du vin, l'avènement de la qualité*. Paris: Éditions Bordas.

European Union Commission. 1999. *CAP Reform: The Wine Sector*. Luxembourg: Office for the Official Publications of the European Communities.

Faith, Nicholas. 1978. *The Winemasters of Bordeaux*. New York: Harper & Row.

Flynn, Julia. 2005. "Grape Expectations: In Napa Valley, Winemaker's Brands Divide an Industry." *Wall Street Journal*, February 22.

Franson, Paul. 2005. "Wine Marketing Companies Increase Roles in Industry." *Wine Business Monthly*, June, 50.

Fredrikson, Jon A. 2001. "The Context for Marketing Strategies: A Look at the US Wine Market." In *Successful Wine Marketing*, ed. K. Moulton and J. Lapsley. Gaithersburg, MD: Aspen Publishers.

Freedman, Alix M., and John R. Emshwiller. 1999. "Vintage System: Big Liquor Wholesaler Finds Change Stalking Its Very Private World." *Wall Street Journal*, October 4.

Gaiter, Dorothy, and John Brecher. 2006. "Organic Wines Make a Natural Progression." *Wall Street Journal*, May 12.

Gautier, Jean-François. 1994. *Les vins de France: Que sais-je?* Paris: Presses Universitaires de France.

Gomberg, Louis R. 1990. "Analytical Perspectives on the California Wine Industry, 1935–1990." Transcript, *Wine Spectator* California Wine Oral History Series, UC Berkeley Regional Oral History Office.

Goode, Jamie. 2005. *The Science of Wine.* Berkeley: University of California Press.

Grgich, Miljenko. 1993. "A Croatian-American Winemaker in the Napa Valley." Transcript, *Wine Spectator* California Wine Oral History Series, UC Berkeley Regional Oral History Office.

Gusfield, Joseph R. 1963. *Symbolic Crusade: Status Politics and the American Temperance Movement.* Urbana: University of Illinois Press.

Hall, C. Michael, Liz Sharples, Brock Cambourne, and Miki Macionis, eds. 2000. *Wine Tourism around the World: Development, Management, and Markets.* Oxford: Butterworth-Heinemann.

Halliday, James. 1994. *A History of the Australian Wine Industry, 1949–1994.* Adelaide: Winetitles.

Heimoff, Steve. 2005. *A Wine Journey along the Russian River.* Berkeley: University of California Press.

Heintz, William F. 1990. *Wine Country: A History of Napa Valley, The Early Years: 1838–1920.* Santa Barbara: Capra Press.

Higounet, Charles. 1993. *Chateau Latour: The History of a Great Vineyard, 1331–1992.* Translated by E. Penning-Rowsell. Kingston-upon-Thames: Seagrave Foulkes.

Hoffman-Martinot, Vincent. 1991. "Grüne and Verts: Two Faces of European Ecologism." *West European Politics* 14 (4): 70–95.

Hutchison, John. 1984. "Northern California from Haraszthy to the Beginnings of Prohibition." In *The University of California/Sotheby Book of California Wine,* ed. Doris Muscatine, Maynard A. Amerine, and Bob Thompson. Berkeley: University of California Press.

Institut National d'Appellations d'Origine. N.d. *L'appellation d'origine contrôlée: Vins et eaux de vie.* Paris: INAO.

Johnson, Hugh. 2005. *A Life Uncorked.* Berkeley: University of California Press.

Kobler, John. 1973. *Ardent Spirits: The Rise and Fall of Prohibition.* New York: Putnam.

Lachiver, Michel. 1988. *Vins, vignes, et vignerons en région parisienne du XVIIe au XIXe siècle.* Paris: Fayard.

Laroche, Michel. 2002. "Mayhem in the Midi." In *Peter Allan Sichel Memorial Lecture.* London: Wine and Spirits Education Trust.

Laube, James. 1999. "Napa's Name down the Drain?" *Wine Spectator,* May 15.

Laube, James, Thomas Garrett, and Mary Ann Worobiec. 1998. "The Vineyard-Designation Trend." *Wine Spectator,* June 15.

LeMay, Marc-Henry. 1995. *Bordeaux et ses vins: Classés par ordre de mérite dans chaque commune.* Bordeaux: Éditions Feret.

Letablier, M.T., and C. Delfosse. 1995. "Genèse d'une convention de qualité: Cas des appellations d'origine fromagères." In *La grande transformation de l'agriculture*, ed. G. Allaire and R. Boyer. Paris: Institut National de la Recherche Agronomique.

Loubère, Leo. *The Red and the White*. Albany: State University of New York, 1978.

Lukacs, Paul. 2000. *Vintage: The Rise of American Wine*. New York: Houghton Mifflin.

Mackay, Jordan. 2005. "Wine's High Stakes Boom Town." *Wine & Spirits*, April, 52–61.

Mansson, Per-Henrik. 2001. "Who Really Controls the Vineyards of France?" *Wine Spectator*, November 30.

Marcus, Kim. 1997. "When Winemakers Become Criminals." *Wine Spectator*, May 15.

Markham, Dewey. 1998. *1855: A History of the Bordeaux Classification*. New York: John Wiley & Sons.

McCoy, Elin. 2005. *The Emperor of Wine: The Rise of Robert M. Parker Jr. and the Reign of American Taste*. New York: Ecco.

McFalls, Laurence. 1990. "In Vino Veritas: Professional Ideology and Politics in Viticultural Languedoc." PhD diss., Harvard University.

McMillan, Rob. 2006. *State of the Wine Industry: Forecast and Strategic Recommendations*. Napa, CA: Silicon Valley Bank.

Mill, John S. 1978 [1859]. *On Liberty*. Indianapolis, IN: Hackett Publishing.

Mondavi, Robert. 1985. "Creativity in the California Wine Industry." Transcript, *Wine Spectator* California Wine Oral History Series, UC Berkeley Regional Oral History Office.

Moone, Michael. 1990. "Management and Marketing at Beringer Vineyards and Wine World, Inc." Transcript, *Wine Spectator* California Wine Oral History Series, UC Berkeley Regional Oral History Office.

Moore, Barrington. 1966. *Social Origins of Dictatorship and Democracy: Lord and Peasant Making in the Modern World*. Boston: Beacon Press.

Muscatine, Doris, Maynard A. Amerine, and Bob Thompson, eds. *The University of California/Sotheby Book of California Wine*. Berkeley: University of California Press, 1984.

Nahoum-Grappe, Véronique. 1995. France. In *International Handbook on Alcohol and Culture*, ed. D.B. Heath. Westport, CT: Greenwood Press.

Onivins. 1999. *Rapport d'activité de la campagne 1998–99*. Paris.

Ostrander, Gilman. 1957. *The Prohibition Movement in California, 1848–1933*. Berkeley: University of California Press.

Parker, Robert M. 1999. *Parker's Wine Buyer's Guide*. New York: Simon and Schuster.

———. 2001. "For What It's Worth." *Wine Advocate*, August, 56.

Penning-Rowsell, Edmund. 1985. *Wines of Bordeaux*. 5th ed. San Francisco: Wine Appreciation Guild.

Pinney, Thomas. 1989. *A History of Wine in America from the Beginnings to Prohibition*. Berkeley: University of California Press.

Prial, Frank J. 2006. "The Wallaby That Roared across the Wine Industry." *New York Times*, April 23, 2006.

Quandt, Richard. 2007. "A Note on a Test for the Sum of Ranksums." *Journal of Wine Economics* 2 (1): 1–5.

Reeve, Jennifer R., L. Carpenter-Boggs, John P. Reganold, Alan L. York, Glenn McGourty, and Leo P. McCloskey. 2005. "Soil and Winegrape Quality in Biodynamically and Organically Managed Vineyards." *American Journal of Enology and Viticulture* 56 (4): 367–76.

Reilly, Jean K. 2004. "Moonshine, Part 2: A Blind Sampling of 20 Wines Shows That Biodynamics Works; But How?" *Fortune*, August 23.

Robinson, Jancis, ed. 1994. *The Oxford Companion to Wine*. Oxford: Oxford University Press.

———, ed. 1999. *The Oxford Companion to Wine*, 2nd ed. Oxford: Oxford University Press.

Roudie, Philippe. 1988. *Vignobles et vignerons du Bordelais*. Bordeaux: Presses Universitaires de Bordeaux.

Rovani, Pierre-Antoine. 2001a. "The 1999 Red Burgundies, Part 1." *Wine Advocate* (135): 43–61.

———. 2001b. "The 1999 Red Burgundies, Part 2." *Wine Advocate* (136): 10–24.

Shelton, Tom. 1999. Statement. In *The Status and Prospects of American Wine Production*, ed. U.H. Hearing before the subcommittee on Livestock and Horticulture. Washington DC.

Skogstad, Grace, and Elizabeth Moore. 2004. "Regulating Genetic Engineering in the United States and the European Union: Policy Development and Policy Resilience." *Politics and Society* 23 (4): 32–56.

Sloan, Frank, Emily Stout, Kathryn Whetten-Goldstein, and Lan Liang. 2000. *Drinkers, Drivers, and Bartenders: Balancing Private Choices and Public Accountability*. Chicago: University of Chicago Press.

Smart, Richard. 2005. "Higher Yields Cause Low Wine Quality." *Wine Business Monthly*, November.

Stiglitz, Joseph E. 1987. The Causes and Consequences of Dependence of Quality on Price. *Journal of Economic Literature* 25 (March): 1–48.

Strong, Rodney. 1994. "Rodney Strong Vineyards: Creative Winemaking and Winery Management in Sonoma County." Transcript, *Wine Spectator* California Wine Oral History Series, UC Berkeley Regional Oral History Office.

Sullivan, Charles L. 1978. "A Viticultural Mystery Solved." *California Historical Society Quarterly* 57 (2): 114–19.

———. 1998. *A Companion to California Wine*. Berkeley: University of California Press.

Taber, George. 1976. "Judgment of Paris." *Time*, June 7.

———. 2005. *Judgment of Paris: California vs. France and the Historic 1976 Paris Tasting That Revolutionized Wine*. New York: Scribner and Son.

Teiser, Ruth, and Catherine Harroun. 1984. "The Volstead Act: Rebirth and Boom." In *The University of California/Sotheby Book of California Wine*, ed. D. Muscatine, M.A. Amerine, and B. Thompson. Berkeley: University of California Press.

Tish, W.R. 2004. "Ten Reasons We All Lose When Numbers Dominate the Marketplace." *Wine Business Monthly*, December.

Trinchero, Louis "Bob." 1992. "California Zinfandels: A Success Story." Transcript, *Wine Spectator* California Wine Oral History Series, UC Berkeley Regional Oral History Office.

Ulin, Robert C. 1996. *Vintages and Traditions: An Ethnohistory of Southwest French Wine Cooperatives.* Washington, DC: Smithsonian Institution.

Unwin, P. H. T. 1991. *Wine and the Vine: An Historical Geography of Viticulture and the Wine Trade.* London: Routledge.

The U.S. Wine Market: Impact Databank, Review, and Forecast. 1998. New York: M. Shanken Communications.

The U.S. Wine Market: Impact Databank, Review, and Forecast. 2005. New York: M. Shanken Communications.

Vogel, David. 1995. *Trading Up: Consumer and Environmental Regulation in a Global Economy.* Cambridge, MA: Harvard University Press.

Warner, Charles K. 1960. *The Winegrowers of France and the Government since 1875.* New York: Columbia University Press.

Weber, Eugen. 1976. *Peasants into Frenchmen.* Stanford, CA: Stanford University Press.

Wilson, James E. 1998. *Terroir: The Role of Geology, Climate, and Culture in the Making of French Wines.* Berkeley: University of California Press.

Winiarski, Warren. 1994. "Creating Classic Wines in the Napa Valley." Transcript, *Wine Spectator* California Wine Oral History Series, UC Berkeley Regional Oral History Office.

Winkler, Albert J. 1966. *General Viticulture.* Berkeley: University of California Press.

Wright, Gordon. 1964. *Rural Revolution in France: The Peasantry in the Twentieth Century.* Stanford, CA: Stanford University Press.

Yandle, Bruce. 1984. "Bootleggers and Baptists." *Regulation* 8 (May–June): 12–16.

Younger, Carolyn. 2006. "Continuing the Fight for the 'Unseen.'" *St. Helena Star,* June 8.

Index

Italicized page numbers refer to illustrations, sidebars, and tables.

Text : 10/13 Sabon
Display : Sabon
Compositor : Aptara
Printer and Binder : Sheridan Book & Journal Services, Inc.